THE OFFICIAL WORLD CUP 2002 FACT FILE

First published by Carlton Books 2002
Copyright © Carlton Books Limited 2002

A CIP catalogue record for this book is available upon request.

ISBN 1 84222 520 0

Project Editor: Martin Corteel
Assistant Editor: David Ballheimer
Senior Art Editor: Darren Jordan
Picture Research: Debora Fioravanti
Production: Sarah Corteel
Design: Simon Mercer

Carlton Books Ltd
20 Mortimer Street
London W1T 3JW

Printed and bound in Italy

Previous page: *Taribo West cuts off a Liberian attack in Nigeria's 2–0 qualifying win in Port Harcourt.*
Above: *Mexico's Carlos Hernandez shoots for goal before South Korea's Myung Hong-bo can tackle in Lyon in 1998.*
Opposite: *Zinedine Zidane lifts the World Cup with his teammates in the Stade de France four years ago.*

THE OFFICIAL  SPORT

WORLD CUP
2002
FACT FILE

CARLTON
BOOKS

CONTENTS

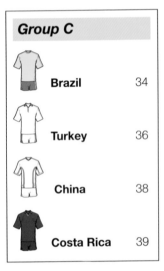
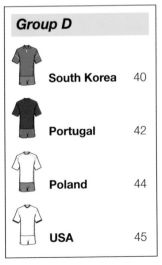
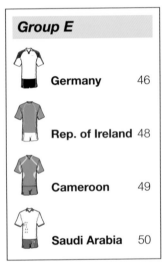
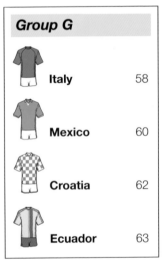
Above: Zinedine Zidane (10) heads home for France against Brazil in the 1998 Final in Saint-Denis.
Opposite: Davor Suker of third-placed Croatia was six-goal top scorer at the 1998 World Cup finals.

INTRODUCTION

The 2002 FIFA World Cup brings football history in its wake. This is the first World Cup of the new century, the first to be staged in Asia and the first to be co-hosted between two nations.

South Korea and Japan were originally competitors for the right to bring the world game's greatest event to the Pacific rim. Then, in the spring of 1996, political pressures within FIFA, the world game's governing body, forced the historic compromise of co-hosting.

The Japanese were bitterly disappointed at having to share the spoils after years of campaigning; the Koreans were delighted that a short, sharp campaign had brought the ultimate reward. Initially, the antagonism of the campaign trail clouded efforts to achieve co-operation. FIFA officials could barely persuade Korean and Japanese officials to agree a date for a meeting, let alone anything more constructive. Eventually, FIFA's then General Secretary, now President, Sepp Blatter's diplomacy brought meetings, discussions, negotiations and then full co-operation at football, security and senior government levels.

The legacy of the 2002 World Cup is likely to reach far beyond football itself while demonstrating the power of the game as a force for good in the world.

The Opening Match will be staged on May 31 in the new World Cup Stadium in Seoul, capital of South Korea. The Final will be hosted by the Yokohama International Stadium in Japan. In between those two matches, the finest players of the top 32 nations in the world will write new pages in the game's own history book.

The World Cup was mooted by FIFA's founding fathers in 1904, but the inaugural event was staged in Uruguay only in 1930, and it has taken place every four years since then, war years excepted. So far 16 tournaments have been held with a steadily increasing entry number reflecting the increasing worldwide passion for the game. Brazil have won the World Cup a record four times, Italy and Germany (West and unified)

Young England fans putting a brave face on their supporting campaign.

on three occasions each, Argentina and Uruguay twice each and England and present holders France once each.

Three countries have played host twice: Italy in 1934 and 1990, France in 1938 and 1998 and Mexico in 1970 and 1986. Six times the hosts have also ended up in triumph: Uruguay in 1930, Italy in 1934, England in 1966, West Germany in 1974,

Newcomers Senegal and their fans will bring a fresh approach to the World Cup finals.

Co-hosting means South Korean fans (inset) can share Japan's pride in the Yokohama International Stadium which hosts the Final.

Argentina in 1978 and France in 1998. Brazil, in 1950, Switzerland (1954), Sweden (1958), Chile (1962), Spain (1982) and USA (1994) were the other hosts.

The World Cup is often compared with the Olympic Games; but the Olympics are built around one city not an entire nation. And not even the Olympics can draw as many billions to their television sets around the globe as the World Cup.

Nor has football been afraid to move with the times. The system of three points for a win, instead of two, was adopted to encourage attacking play. A crackdown has been undertaken by referees against the so-called "professional foul" and against time-wasting and the feigning of injury. The game has opened its mind to the value of experimentation with new ideas.

Co-hosting is perhaps the most intriguing of all.

Political differences were set aside when the USA played Iran at Lyon in France 98.

THE DRAW DIPLOMACY RULES

Newcomers Senegal were granted the highest-profile role of all when the World Cup finals draw, in Busan, south-east Korea, matched them with holders France in the Opening Match in Group A in Seoul.

The greatest pre-draw fuss centred, as always, on the identity of the eight top seeds. The holders and hosts are always among them, thus granting the hosts the right to start in the venue of their choice. Modern World Cup tradition decided four of the five nations to join France, South Korea and Japan in the top eight – that meant four-times winners Brazil, three-times winners Italy and Germany and double winners Argentina.

A complex computation of recent qualifying records plus the FIFA rankings decided that Spain should complete the top eight in a draw which was choreographed as carefully as the dance routines which enlivened the occasion for the worldwide television audience. The next two in the rating coefficient were Mexico and England.

Group A is completed by twice-winners Uruguay and former European champions Denmark. The Danes thrashed Uruguay 6–1 in Mexico in 1986 but doubt the prospects of such a repeat. Group B matches Spain with Paraguay – who eliminated the Spaniards in the first round in 1998 – with relative international freshmen Slovenia and South Africa. South Africa were new to the World Cup finals at France 98 while Slovenia entered the international stratosphere at Euro 2000.

Brazil landed what appeared the easiest draw – with the inadvertent and embarrassed assistance of Pele – in Group C, challenged by improving Turkey, Costa Rica and China. Intriguingly, China coach Bora Milutinovic had been boss of Costa Rica on their only other appearance in the finals, in 1990, when they lost only 1–0 to Brazil in a first-round group match.

Co-hosts face tough tests

Group D will attract particular attention because of the co-hosts Korea, though Portugal, Euro 2000 semi-finalists and starring Luis Figo, will be favourites to win the section. Poland were superb in qualifying but lack top-level experience compared with the United States, who will be appearing in the finals for the fourth consecutive time.

Germany bring almost unmatched experience of the World Cup challenge to Group E, wary of the commitment of the Republic of Ireland. Olympic champions Cameroon and Saudi Arabia, completing a hat-trick of finals appearances, are confident of upsetting European ambitions.

Group F, with Argentina, Nigeria, England and Sweden was described by Nigerian coach Amodu Shaibu as the "Zone of Death". Argentina ran away with the South American qualifying section while England topped European Group Nine in erratic style. Neither will expect any gifts along the way from Nigeria or Sweden, who were third as recently as 1994.

Three-times winners Italy and Croatia, third last time, are the European heavyweights in Group G preparing for a straight duel with Latin America, represented by Mexico and Ecuador. Ecuador make their finals debut.

Group H matches co-hosts Japan with Belgium, Russia and Tunisia. Japan are learning all the time and coach Pierre Troussier has World Cup finals experience with South Africa and an excellent playmaker in Hidetoshi Nakata.

At the end of the show, the draw had achieved its aim of balancing out the world's top nations. Seven of the eight groups comprise representatives from three different regions while Group C, with Brazil, Turkey, Costa Rica and China, boasts four – from South America, Europe, Central America and Asia, respectively.

Left: *FIFA secretary Michel Zen-Ruffinen holds up England during the draw for the 2002 World Cup.*

Opposite: *Anastacia performs the Official World Cup Song for the first time.*

THE VENUES

The 2002 World Cup will be breaking new ground in many ways. The competition is being staged in Asia across two countries, a record 20 stadiums will host matches and 19 of them are less than five years old. Never before have any of these happened.

Proof of FIFA's dream to expand the World Cup into a truly global event has never been more vividly brought to life than by this competition. Football was not a national sport in Japan until the 1990s, but they are now soccer-mad. South Korea are the most successful of all Asian nations in terms of World Cup finals qualification. These two

super-powers of the AFC (Asian Football Confederation) are sure to make the 2002 World Cup a party to remember.

But whatever happens on the pitch, one thing will stand out as exceptional in 2002: the venues. The oldest 2002 World Cup stadium in South Korea will be 14 months old when the tournament opens. And, maybe

even more amazingly, the design and architecture of each of them is different. From the "old-fashioned" four-stands design of Kobe to the futuristic "bird's-wing" roof of Suwon or the "boomerang" roof of Miyagi, these stadiums are very special.

Maps of South Korea and Japan showing the 20 venues to be used during the month-long tournament.

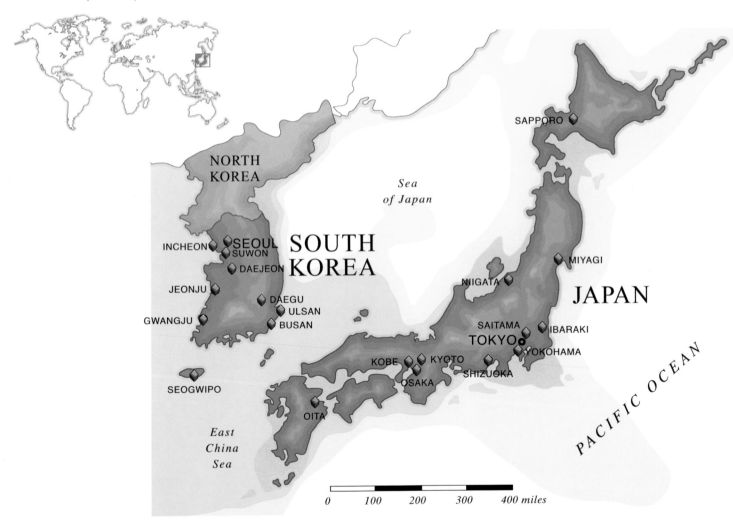

KOREA

Seoul *World Cup Stadium*
Constructed: *December 2001* **Capacity:** *64,677*
Matches: *Opening game, group match, semi-final*

Seoul, the capital of Korea, will host the opening ceremony on 31 May, with the holders, France, kicking off the tournament against Senegal. The World Cup Stadium, in the new Millennium City suburb

of Seoul, opened on 10 November 2001. Its capacity of 64,677 is the largest for any soccer-only stadium in Asia. The city of Seoul was the centrepiece of the 1988 Summer Olympic Games, but the multi-sport Chamsil Stadium – itself constructed for the event – was beginning to show its age, so it was decided to start again. Built on reclaimed land, the authorities envisage inviting high-tech companies to set up their HQs in the new town. The World Cup Stadium's first match saw South Korea play against 2002 qualifiers Croatia, who stepped in at short notice in place of Germany, who were involved in a qualification play-off against Ukraine.

Busan *Sports Complex Main Stadium*
Constructed: *July 2001* **Capacity:** *55,982*
Matches: *3 group matches*

With a population of four million, Busan is Korea's second largest city and is recognized as one of the world's three largest seaports. Busan is also a big sporting city. It has hosted the 1986 Asian Games, as well as the football and yachting competitions of the 1988 Olympic Games and the 1997 East Asian Games.

Daegu *Main Stadium*
Constructed: May 2001 Capacity: 66,040
Matches: 3 group matches, third-place play-off

Opened in May 2001 and situated in the Suseonggu district of Korea's largest textile and fashion-making city, Daegu Main Stadium took just under four years to build. Of the 66,040 seats, 74 per-cent are covered by a Teflon coating roof membrane that lets through natural light to create a comfortable environment for spectators. The roof's design imitates the beautiful curves of a traditional Korean house with a straw-thatched roof.

Daejeon *World Cup Stadium*
Constructed: September 2001 Capacity: 42,407
Matches: 2 group matches, 1 second round

Daejeon, 150 kilometres south-east of Seoul, is known as Korea's Silicon Valley. It is also a major transportation hub. For visitors coming to Daejeon for the World Cup who want to get a first-hand experience of Korean life, nearly 400 households have offered to make home-stay arrangements.

Gwangju *World Cup Stadium*
Constructed: September 2001 Capacity: 42,880
Matches: 2 group matches, 1 quarter-final

Gwangju's long-cherished love of the arts is highlighted by Gwangju Biennale, an arts festival growing in world renown, and the city plans to link World Cup 2002 with a fourth edition of the Biennale. Gwangju has also signed an agreement for extensive exchanges in sports, culture, and other fields with Sendai, a city in the Miyagi region – one of Japan's World Cup venues.

Incheon *Munhak Stadium*
Constructed: December 2001 Capacity: 52,256
Matches: 3 group matches

Incheon, Korea's second largest port, is just 28 kilometres west of Seoul and is expanding to become one of Asia's main travel hubs. The Munhak Stadium opened in December 2001.

Jeonju *World Cup Stadium*
Constructed: September 2001 Capacity: 42,477
Matches: 2 group matches, 1 second round

Jeonju – with a history dating back 1300 years – is notable for the largest Korean-style house village, with over 800 households, and it is preserved as a special folk culture zone. The stadium is beautiful. Its four concave roofs form a symbolic fan hanging on suspension cables that represent the 12 strings of a Gaya harp, a Korean musical instrument.

Seogwipo *World Cup Stadium*
Constructed: December 2001 Capacity: 42,256
Matches: 2 group matches, 1 second round

Seogwipo is located on the country's largest island, Jeju-do, south of the Korean Peninsula. It is a popular destination for tourists, and tourism is a leading industry. Jeju-do has also hosted high level political summits.

Suwon *World Cup Stadium*
Constructed: May 2001 Capacity: 43,138
Matches: 3 group matches, 1 second round

Suwon provides a blend of high-tech industry and tourism. The city is building the Suwon Convention Centre, the Image Theme Park, the World's Miniature Castle Park and the Hwasong Observation Tower. The stadium – which will become the home of Korea's top club, Samsung Blue Wings – also has a multi-purpose cultural centre, with swimming pools, tennis courts, cinemas and concert halls.

Ulsan *Munsu Soccer Stadium*
Constructed: April 2001 Capacity: 43,512
Matches: 2 group matches, 1 quarter-final

Munsu Stadium, at Ulsan, has two levels below ground and three above. In an environment of natural ponds and thick forests on nearby mountains, it is one of the most beautiful venues of the 2002 World Cup. The architects created the stadium to represent the image of a crane – the symbol of Ulsan – crouching before taking flight.

JAPAN

Yokohama *International Sports Stadium*
Constructed: October 1997 Capacity: 70,574
Matches: 3 group matches, Final

Yokohama, 30 minutes by road from Tokyo, is Japan's second largest city. The stadium is the second oldest of all the 2002 World Cup finals venues and it is less than five years old! With a capacity of 70,000, it has the largest capacity of all the stadia and it is fitting that it should stage the Final. Yokohama International is the home of J. League team, the Marinos.

Ibaraki *Kashima Football Stadium*
Constructed: May 2001 Capacity: 41,800 Matches: 3 group matches

Football plays a large part in the life of Kashima City in Ibaraki prefecture. The stadium can accommodate over two-thirds of the city's population and as fans approach it, they will be greeted by a bronze statue of legendary Brazilian player Zico, who led the Kashima Antlers to J. League championships in the 1990s.

Kobe *Wing Stadium*
Constructed: October 2001 Capacity: 42,000
Matches: 2 group matches, 1 second round

Kobe dates back to the eighth century, but the 20th century was cruel to the city. It was devastated during World War II, losing two-thirds of its million-plus population. Then, having recovered and been rebuilt, the 1995 Hanshin Awaji earthquake destroyed it again. The beautiful Kobe Wing Stadium was so named to conjure up the image of wings, rising from the reconstruction after the earthquake.

Miyagi *Miyagi Stadium*

Constructed: March 2000 Capacity: 49,133
Matches: 2 group matches, 1 second round

State-of-the-art Miyagi Stadium pays homage to the region's historical heritage with an innovative design combining the traditional and the modern. It features a sweeping crescent-shaped grandstand reminiscent of the headpiece worn on the battle dress helmet of the ruling Date clan during Japan's feudal period.

Niigata *Niigata Stadium*

Constructed: March 2001 Capacity: 42,700
Matches: 2 group matches, 1 second round

Surrounded by mountains, dotted by interior plateaus, Niigata was once a remote and inaccessible area of Japan. Now, Niigata Prefectural Stadium is close to rail and air links. The stadium's finest feature is its translucent white roof, which allows in 80 percent natural light and stretches across 90 percent of the seating. The curves of the roof have been compared with an image of swans alighting on the nearby Toyanogata lagoon.

Oita *Oita Stadium*

Constructed: March 2001 Capacity: 43,000
Matches: 2 group matches, 1 second round

The prefecture of Oita is famous for its spa resorts. However, after the World Cup finals, it may be better known for the amazing "Big Eye" stadium. Viewed from the air, it looks like a giant eye, whether the retractable roof is open or closed.

Osaka *Nagai Stadium*

Renovation: May 1996 Capacity: 50,000
Matches: 2 group matches, 1 quarter-final

Known as "the City of Waters", Osaka has been a commercial centre since the Middle Ages. Japan's third-largest city, Osaka's businesses have laid the groundwork for a modern urban infrastructure and rich cultural traditions. Nagai Stadium is the oldest in use for the finals.

Saitama *Soccer Stadium*

Constructed: July 2001 Capacity: 63,700
Matches: 3 group matches, 1 semi-final

Uruwa City, in Saitama prefecture, is almost a suburb of Tokyo, being just 24 kilometres north of the capital. It is another soccer-mad region, boasting the Urawa Red Diamonds, whose fans are considered the most enthusiastic in Japan. The stadium is the largest football-only facility in Japan and is another marvel of modern architecture.

Sapporo *Sapporo Dome*

Constructed: June 2001 Capacity: 42,122
Matches: 3 group matches

Viewed from ground level, the Sapporo Dome resembles a science fiction spacecraft. It's not a bad allusion, because its grass pitch can be wheeled into and out of the Dome, a truly futuristic concept. Sapporo, on Hokkaido Island, has hosted major sporting events before, most notably the 1972 Winter Olympic Games.

Shizuoka *Stadium Ecopa*

Constructed: March 2001 Capacity: 51,349
Matches: 2 group matches, 1 quarter-final

Shizuoka Stadium Ecopa nestles in an area of gentle hills in the western part of Shizuoka prefecture, the region famous for Mount Fuji and green tea. The stadium exterior is designed to reflect the beauty of the Ogasayama Mountains nearby. The main feature of the newly-created Ogasayama Sports Park it has over 5,000 retractable seats to move spectators on to the surrounding athletics track and closer to the football pitch.

THE FIXTURES

Chart the progress of the 2002 FIFA World Cup finals on these two pages so that, when the final whistle blows at the end of the Final (or the penalty shoot-out), you will have a record of all the vital happenings.

In the First Round, there are eight groups of four countries, from which the first two will advance to the knock-out stages. Space has been left for you to fill in each result and at the end of the First Round, to complete the league tables for the groups. From the Second Round (round of 16) on, the competition is a straight knock-out. If the scores are level after 90 minutes, the games will go into extra-time. The first goal of extra-time, the golden goal, wins the matchbut if neither team scores, the tie will be decided by penalty kicks.

The system for the shoot-out is five kicks per team, taken alternately, unless one has an unbeatable lead after three or four penalties. If the teams remain level after five penalty kicks, then it goes to sudden-death. In sudden-death, the teams continue in alternate order, and the match is decided as soon as one team scores in one round and the other fails.

All kick-off times are local.

FIRST ROUND

GROUP A

Date	(Time)	Venue	Fixture	Score
May 31	(20:30)	Seoul	**France vs. Senegal**	.....–.....
June 1	(18:00)	Ulsan	**Uruguay vs. Denmark**	.....–.....
June 6	(15:30)	Busan	**France vs. Uruguay**	.....–.....
June 6	(20:30)	Daegu	**Denmark vs. Senegal**	.....–.....
June 11	(15:30)	Incheon	**Denmark vs. France**	.....–.....
June 11	(15:30)	Suwon	**Senegal vs. Uruguay**	.....–.....

GROUP A FINAL TABLE

Team	P	W	D	L	F	A	Pts
1							
2							
3							
4							

GROUP B

Date	(Time)	Venue	Fixture	Score
June 2	(16:30)	Busan	**Paraguay vs. South Africa**	.....–.....
June 2	(20:30)	Gwangju	**Spain vs. Slovenia**	.....–.....
June 7	(18:00)	Jeonju	**Spain vs. Paraguay**	.....–.....
June 8	(15:30)	Daegu	**South Africa vs. Slovenia**	.....–.....
June 12	(15:30)	Daejeon	**South Africa vs. Spain**	.....–.....
June 12	(15:30)	Seogwipo	**Slovenia vs. Paraguay**	.....–.....

GROUP B FINAL TABLE

Team	P	W	D	L	F	A	Pts
1							
2							
3							
4							

GROUP C

Date	(Time)	Venue	Fixture	Score
June 3	(18:00)	Ulsan	**Brazil vs. Turkey**	.....–.....
June 4	(15:30)	Gwangju	**China vs. Costa Rica**	.....–.....
June 8	(20:30)	Seogwipo	**Brazil vs. China**	.....–.....
June 9	(18:00)	Incheon	**Costa Rica vs. Turkey**	.....–.....
June 13	(15:30)	Suwon	**Costa Rica vs. Brazil**	.....–.....
June 13	(15:30)	Seoul	**Turkey vs. China**	.....–.....

GROUP C FINAL TABLE

Team	P	W	D	L	F	A	Pts
1							
2							
3							
4							

GROUP D

Date	(Time)	Venue	Fixture	Score
June 4	(20:30)	Busan	**South Korea vs. Poland**	.....–.....
June 5	(18:00)	Suwon	**USA vs. Portugal**	.....–.....
June 10	(15:30)	Daegu	**South Korea vs. USA**	.....–.....
June 10	(20:30)	Jeonju	**Portugal vs. Poland**	.....–.....
June 14	(20:30)	Incheon	**Portugal vs. South Korea**	.....–.....
June 14	(20:30)	Daejeon	**Poland vs. USA**	.....–.....

GROUP D FINAL TABLE

Team	P	W	D	L	F	A	Pts
1							
2							
3							
4							

GROUP E

Date	(Time)	Venue	Fixture	Score
June 1	(15:30)	Niigata	**Rep of Ire vs. Cameroon**	.....–.....
June 1	(20:30)	Sapporo	**Germany vs. Saudi Arabia**	.....–.....
June 5	(20:30)	Ibaraki	**Germany vs. Rep of Ire**	.....–.....
June 6	(18:00)	Saitama	**Cameroon vs. Saudi Arabia**	.....–.....
June 11	(20:30)	Shizuoka	**Cameroon vs. Germany**	.....–.....
June 11	(20:30)	Yokohama	**Saudi Arabia vs. Rep of Ire**	.....–.....

GROUP E FINAL TABLE

Team	P	W	D	L	F	A	Pts
1							
2							
3							
4							

GROUP F

Date	(Time)	Venue	Fixture	Score
June 2	(14:30)	Saitama	**England vs. Sweden**	.....–.....
June 2	(18:30)	Ibaraki	**Argentina vs. Nigeria**	.....–.....
June 7	(15:30)	Kobe	**Sweden vs. Nigeria**	.....–.....
June 7	(20:30)	Sapporo	**Argentina vs. England**	.....–.....
June 12	(15:30)	Miyagi	**Sweden vs. Argentina**	.....–.....
June 12	(15:30)	Osaka	**Nigeria vs. England**	.....–.....

GROUP F FINAL TABLE

Team	P	W	D	L	F	A	Pts
1							
2							
3							
4							

FIRST ROUND continued

GROUP G

Date	(Time)	Venue	Fixture	Score
June 3	(15:30)	Niigata	Croatia vs. Mexico	.....−.....
June 3	(20:30)	Sapporo	Italy vs. Ecuador	.....−.....
June 8	(18:00)	Ibaraki	Italy vs. Croatia	.....−.....
June 9	(15:30)	Miyagi	Mexico vs. Ecuador	.....−.....
June 13	(20:30)	Oita	Mexico vs. Italy	.....−.....
June 13	(20:30)	Yokohama	Ecuador vs. Croatia	.....−.....

GROUP G FINAL TABLE

Team		P	W	D	L	F	A	Pts
1								
2								
3								
4								

GROUP H

Date	(Time)	Venue	Fixture	Score
June 4	(18:00)	Saitama	Japan vs. Belgium	.....−.....
June 5	(15:30)	Kobe	Russia vs. Tunisia	.....−.....
June 9	(20:30)	Yokohama	Japan vs. Russia	.....−.....
June 10	(18:00)	Oita	Tunisia vs. Belgium	.....−.....
June 14	(15:30)	Osaka	Tunisia vs. Japan	.....−.....
June 14	(15:30)	Shizuoka	Belgium vs. Russia	.....−.....

GROUP H FINAL TABLE

Team		P	W	D	L	F	A	Pts
1								
2								
3								
4								

LAST SIXTEEN

June 15, Seogwipo (15:30)
Winner Group E vs. **Runner-up Group B**

June 15, Niigata (20:30)
Winner Group A vs. **Runner-up Group F**

June 16, Oita (15:30)
Winner Group F vs. **Runner-up Group A**

June 16, Suwon (20:30)
Winner Group B vs. **Runner-up Group E**

June 17, Jeonju (15:30)
Winner Group G vs. **Runner-up Group D**

June 17, Kobe (20:30)
Winner Group C vs. **Runner-up Group H**

June 18, Miyagi (15:30)
Winner Group H vs. **Runner-up Group C**

June 18, Daejon (20:30)
Winner Group D vs. **Runner-up Group G**

QUARTER-FINALS

June 21, Shizuoka (15:30)
Winner Niigata vs. **Winner Kobe**

June 21, Ulsan (20:30)
Winner Seogwipo vs. **Winner Jeonju**

June 22, Gwangju (15:30)
Winner Suwon vs. **Winner Daejon**

June 22, Osaka (20:30)
Winner Oita vs. **Winner Miyagi**

SEMI-FINALS

June 25, Seoul (20:30)
Winner Ulsan vs. **Winner Gwangju**

June 26, Saitama (20:30)
Winner Shizuoka vs. **Winner Osaka**

THIRD/FOURTH PLACE PLAY-OFF **June 29, Daegu** (20:00)

Loser Seoul vs. **Loser Saitama**

FINAL **June 30, Yokahama** (20:00)

Winner Seoul vs. **Winner Saitama**

Scorers | *Scorers*

HOW THEY QUALIFIED

The launchpad for a record-breaking World Cup came in March 2000 with 196 nations around the globe looking to join hosts South Korea and Japan and champions France in the finals. By the end of November 2001, 788 matches – in front of an aggregate 16 million fans – had been played and the last 32 were in place.

Neither of the two nations who kicked off the 2002 World Cup qualifying tournament reached the finals. The "real" opening match of the 2002 event was played in Port of Spain on 4 March 2000, when Trinidad and Tobago beat Netherlands Antilles 5–0. Marvin Andrews scored the first goal after 19 minutes and Eugene Martha of the Netherlands Antilles saw the first red card after 58 minutes.

Africa was the first continent to complete its qualifying competition. By the end of July 2001, some 10 months before the finals, Olympic champions Cameroon, Nigeria, newcomers Senegal, South Africa and Tunisia had secured their tickets.

From North and Central America and Caribbean confederation, the United States and Mexico, as expected, qualified but both made hard work of it, as reviving Costa Rica topped the group and Honduras narrowly missed out.

Saudi Arabia and finals debutants China, under the World Cup's managerial magician, Bora Milutinovic, came through from Asia with Iran defeating the United Arab Emirates in a regional play-off for the right to play off again. This time they lost, to the Irish Republic.

The Irish had been the odd men out after a nine-group European section from which the winners went direct to the finals and the runners-up played off against one other. Poland and Sweden were the first to qualify, closely followed by Russia, Portugal, Denmark, Croatia, Spain, Italy and England. Former winners Germany ultimately made it through the play-offs along with Belgium, newcomers Slovenia and Turkey.

In South America, Argentina raced away at the top of the group pursued at some distance by Paraguay and first-time qualifiers Ecuador. Brazil, amid worldwide consternation, went through no fewer than three coaches as they staggered into the fourth and last direct qualifying slot.

Uruguay finished fifth and had to beat Oceania winners Australia 3–1 on aggregate to clinch the 29th and last qualifying slot – some 20 months after it had all begun. Australia had set all sorts of records reaching the last qualifying stage, recording world-best 31–0 and 22–0 victories over American Samoa and Tonga, respectively.

Alvaro Recoba of Uruguay is on top of the world after Uruguay's play-off victory over Australia in Montevide allowed the former world champions to snatch the last available slot in the finals.

ASIA

First round of 10 groups (finishing order to the right). Group winners advanced to the second (final) round in two groups of five. The two group winners qualified directly for the World Cup finals; the two runners-up (Iran and United Arab Emirates) met and the winners of this regional play-off (Iran) faced UEFA group runner-up (Republic of Ireland). The winner of this play-off (Republic of Ireland) advanced to the World Cup finals.

Group 1: **Oman**, Syria, Laos, Philippines
Group 2: **Iran**, Tajikistan, Guam
Group 3: **Qatar**, Palestine, Malaysia, Hong Kong
Group 4: **Bahrain**, Kuwait, Kyrgyzstan, Singapore
Group 5: **Thailand**, Lebanon, Sri Lanka, Pakistan
Group 6: **Iraq**, Kazakhstan, Nepal, Macao
Group 7: **Uzbekistan**, Turkmenistan, Jordan, Chinese Taipei
Group 8: **United Arab Emirates**, Yemen, India, Brunei Darussalam
Group 9: **China PR**, Indonesia, Maldives Republic, Cambodia
Group 10: **Saudi Arabia**, Vietnam SR, Bangladesh, Mongolia

GROUP A

Team	P	W	D	L	GF	GA	Pts
Saudi Arabia	**8**	**5**	**2**	**1**	**17**	**8**	**17**
Iran	*8*	*4*	*3*	*1*	*10*	*7*	*15*
Bahrain	8	2	4	2	8	9	10
Iraq	8	2	1	5	9	10	7
Thailand	8	0	4	4	5	15	4

GROUP B

Team	P	W	D	L	GF	GA	Pts
China PR	**8**	**6**	**1**	**1**	**13**	**2**	**19**
United Arab Emirates	*8*	*3*	*2*	*3*	*10*	*11*	*11*
Uzbekistan	8	3	1	4	13	14	10
Qatar	8	2	3	3	10	10	9
Oman	8	1	3	4	7	16	6

AFC PLAY-OFF

Iran vs. United Arab Emirates	1–0, 3–0

AFRICA

First round played on a two-legged basis. The winners advanced to second round of groups and the five second round group winners advanced to the World Cup finals.

Guinea-Bissau vs. **Togo**	0–0, 0–3
Mauritania vs. **Tunisia**	1–2, 0–3
Benin vs. **Senegal**	1–1, 0–1
Gambia vs. **Morocco**	0–1, 0–2
Cape Verde Islands vs. **Algeria**	0–0, 0–2
Botswana vs. **Zambia**	0–1, 0–1
Sudan vs. Mozambique	1–0, 1–2
Lesotho vs. **South Africa**	0–2, 0–1
Madagascar vs. Gabon	2–0, 0–1
Swaziland vs. **Angola**	0–1, 1–7
Sao Tome e Principe vs. **Sierra Leone**	2–0, 0–4
Rwanda vs. **Cote d'Ivoire**	2–2, 0–2
Libya vs. Mali	3–0, 1–3

Central African Rep. vs. **Zimbabwe**	0–1, 1–3
Equatorial Guinea vs. **Congo**	1–3, 1–2
Somalia vs. **Cameroon**	0–3, 0–3
Djibouti vs. **Congo DR**	1–1, 1–9
Mauritius vs. **Egypt**	0–2, 2–4
Eritrea vs. **Nigeria**	0–0, 0–4
Seychelles vs. **Namibia**	1–1, 0–3
Uganda vs. **Guinea**	4–4, 0–3
Ethiopia vs. **Burkina Faso**	2–1, 0–3
Malawi vs. Kenya	2–0, 0–0
Tanzania vs. **Ghana**	0–1, 2–3
Chad vs. **Liberia**	0–1, 0–0

CAF GROUP A

Team	P	W	D	L	GF	GA	Pts.
Cameroon	**8**	**6**	**1**	**1**	**14**	**4**	**19**
Angola	8	3	4	1	11	9	13
Zambia	8	3	2	3	14	11	11
Togo	8	2	3	3	10	13	9
Libya	8	0	2	6	7	19	2

CAF GROUP B

Team	P	W	D	L	GF	GA	Pts.
Nigeria	**8**	**5**	**1**	**2**	**15**	**3**	**16**
Liberia	8	5	0	3	10	8	15
Sudan	8	4	0	4	8	10	12
Ghana	8	3	2	3	10	9	11
Sierra Leone	8	1	1	6	2	15	4

CAF GROUP C

Team	P	W	D	L	GF	GA	Pts
Senegal	**8**	**4**	**3**	**1**	**14**	**2**	**15**
Morocco	8	4	3	1	8	3	15
Egypt	8	3	4	1	16	7	13
Algeria	8	2	2	4	11	14	8
Namibia	8	0	2	6	3	26	2

CAF GROUP D

Team	P	W	D	L	GF	GA	Pts.
Tunisia	**8**	**6**	**2**	**0**	**23**	**4**	**20**
Côte d'Ivoire	8	4	3	1	18	8	15
Congo DR	8	3	1	4	7	16	10
Madagascar	8	2	0	6	5	15	6
Congo	8	1	2	5	5	15	5

CAF GROUP E

Team	P	W	D	L	GF	GA	Pts
South Africa	**6**	**5**	**1**	**0**	**10**	**3**	**16**
Zimbabwe	6	4	0	2	7	5	12
Burkina Faso	6	1	2	3	7	8	5
Malawi	6	0	1	5	4	12	1

Guinea were suspended after playing four matches and their record was expunged.

CONCACAF — NORTH AND CENTRAL AMERICA, CARIBBEAN

CONCACAF had the most complicated and convoluted qualifying competition. One nation (Canada) received a bye into the Caribbean/Central American playoffs, while four others (Costa Rica, Jamaica, Mexico and USA) received byes directly into the semi-finals. The first round was split into three Caribbean divisions and two Central America divisions. In the three Caribbean divisions

each team played two rounds of two-legged knock-out matches before a section final. The winners of this two-legged match went into one of three semi-final groups; the losers had a second chance in the Caribbean/Central American playoffs. The Central American section was split into two three-team groups with the winners advancing to the semi-finals, the second place team going into the

Caribbean/Central American playoffs. The Caribbean/Central American playoffs were two-legged matches with the winners advancing to the semi-finals. The first and second teams from each of the three semi-final groups advanced to the CONCACAF group finals (Costa Rica after a one-game play-off), a six-team round robin competition. The top three went to the World Cup finals.

Caribbean 1 qualifiers:
Barbados
(playoff *Cuba*)

Caribbean 2 qualifiers:
St Vincent & Grenadines
(playoff *Antigua and Barbuda*)

Caribbean 3 qualifiers:
Trinidad & Tobago
(playoff *Haiti*)

Central America qualifiers:
El Salvador and **Panama**
(playoffs *Guatemala* and *Honduras*)

Playoff winners:
Canada, Guatemala
and **Honduras**

CONCACAF Semifinals – GROUP C

Team	P	W	D	L	GF	GA	Pts
Trinidad & Tobago	6	5	0	1	14	7	15
Mexico	6	4	1	1	17	2	13
Canada	6	1	2	3	1	8	5
Panama	6	0	1	5	1	16	1

CONCACAF Semifinals – GROUP D

Team	P	W	D	L	GF	GA	Pts
Honduras	6	5	0	1	25	5	15
Jamaica	6	4	0	2	7	4	12
El Salvador	6	3	0	3	13	13	9
St Vincent & Grenadines	6	0	0	6	2	25	0

CONCACAF Semifinals – GROUP E

Team	P	W	D	L	GF	GA	Pts
United States	6	3	2	1	14	3	11
Costa Rica	6	3	1	2	9	6	10
Guatemala	6	3	1	2	9	6	10
Barbados	6	1	0	5	3	20	3

PLAY-OFF

Costa Rica vs. Guatemala 5–2

CONCACAF Finals

Team	P	W	D	L	GF	GA	Pts
Costa Rica	10	7	2	1	17	7	23
Mexico	10	5	2	3	16	9	17
United States	10	5	2	3	11	8	17
Honduras	10	4	2	4	17	17	14
Jamaica	10	2	2	6	7	14	8
Trinidad and Tobago	10	1	2	7	5	18	5

Cuauhtemoc Blanco delights the Azteca Stadium by striking one of his two goals in Mexico's concluding qualifying tie against Honduras.

UEFA

The UEFA qualifying competition was relatively straightforward. Nine groups of five or six nations played a round-robin tournament, with the group winners qualifying directly for the World Cup finals. Eight runners-up played off over two legs for four more teams to advance to the finals. The other second-place team (Republic of Ireland) faced a team from Asia (Iran) with the winner going to Japan/Korea.

GROUP 1

Team	P	W	D	L	GF	GA	Pts
Russia	**10**	**7**	**2**	**1**	**18**	**5**	**23**
Slovenia	*10*	*5*	*5*	*0*	*17*	*9*	*20*
Yugoslavia	10	5	4	1	22	8	19
Switzerland	10	4	2	4	18	12	14
Faroe Islands	10	2	1	7	6	23	7
Luxembourg	10	0	0	10	4	28	0

GROUP 2

Team	P	W	D	L	GF	GA	Pts
Portugal	**10**	**7**	**3**	**0**	**33**	**7**	**24**
Republic of Ireland	*10*	*7*	*3*	*0*	*23*	*5*	*24*
Holland	10	6	2	2	30	9	20
Estonia	10	2	2	6	10	26	8
Cyprus	10	2	2	6	13	31	8
Andorra	10	0	0	10	5	36	0

GROUP 3

Team	P	W	D	L	GF	GA	Pts
Denmark	**10**	**6**	**4**	**0**	**22**	**6**	**22**
Czech Republic	*10*	*6*	*2*	*2*	*20*	*8*	*20*
Bulgaria	10	5	2	3	14	15	17
Iceland	10	4	1	5	14	20	13
Northern Ireland	10	3	2	5	11	12	11
Malta	10	0	1	9	4	24	1

GROUP 4

Team	P	W	D	L	GF	GA	Pts
Sweden	**10**	**8**	**2**	**0**	**20**	**3**	**26**
Turkey	*10*	*6*	*3*	*1*	*18*	*8*	*21*
Slovakia	10	5	2	3	16	9	17
Macedonia FYR	10	1	4	5	11	18	7
Moldova	10	1	3	6	6	20	6
Azerbaijan	10	1	2	7	4	17	5

GROUP 5

Team	P	W	D	L	GF	GA	Pts
Poland	**10**	**6**	**3**	**1**	**21**	**11**	**21**
Ukraine	*10*	*4*	*5*	*1*	*13*	*8*	*17*
Belarus	10	4	3	3	12	11	15
Norway	10	2	4	4	12	14	10
Wales	10	1	6	3	10	12	9
Armenia	10	0	5	5	7	19	5

GROUP 6

Team	P	W	D	L	GF	GA	Pts
Croatia	**8**	**5**	**3**	**0**	**15**	**2**	**18**
Belgium	*8*	*5*	*2*	*1*	*25*	*6*	*17*
Scotland	8	4	3	1	12	6	15
Latvia	8	1	1	6	5	16	4
San Marino	8	0	1	7	3	30	1

GROUP 7

Team	P	W	D	L	GF	GA	Pts
Spain	**8**	**6**	**2**	**0**	**21**	**4**	**20**
Austria	*8*	*4*	*3*	*1*	*10*	*8*	*15*
Israel	8	3	3	2	11	7	12
Bosnia-Herzegovina	8	2	2	4	12	12	8
Liechtenstein	8	0	0	8	0	23	0

GROUP 8

Team	P	W	D	L	GF	GA	Pts
Italy	**8**	**6**	**2**	**0**	**16**	**3**	**20**
Romania	*8*	*5*	*1*	*2*	*10*	*7*	*16*
Georgia	8	3	1	4	12	12	10
Hungary	8	2	2	4	14	13	8
Lithuania	8	0	2	6	3	20	2

GROUP 9

Team	P	W	D	L	GF	GA	Pts
England	**8**	**5**	**2**	**1**	**16**	**6**	**17**
Germany	*8*	*5*	*2*	*1*	*14*	*10*	*17*
Finland	8	3	3	2	12	7	12
Greece	8	2	1	5	7	17	7
Albania	8	1	0	7	5	14	3

PLAY-OFFS

Slovenia vs. Romania	2–1, 1–1	**Belgium** vs. Czech Republic	1–0, 1–0	**Republic of Ireland** vs. Iran	2–0, 0–1
Ukraine vs. **Germany**	1–1, 1–4	Austria vs. **Turkey**	0–1, 0–5	

SOUTH AMERICA

CONMEBOL had the most straightforward of all the qualifying competitions – all 10 nations were in one league, playing home and away against the other nine. The top four teams advanced directly to the World Cup finals, while the fifth-placed nation (Uruguay) played against the Oceania winners (Australia).

Team	P	W	D	L	GF	GA	Pts
Argentina	**18**	**13**	**4**	**1**	**42**	**15**	**43**
Ecuador	**18**	**9**	**4**	**5**	**23**	**20**	**31**
Brazil	**18**	**9**	**3**	**6**	**31**	**17**	**30**
Paraguay	**18**	**9**	**3**	**6**	**29**	**23**	**30**
Uruguay	*18*	*7*	*6*	*5*	*19*	*13*	*27*
Colombia	18	7	6	5	20	15	27
Bolivia	18	4	6	8	21	33	18
Peru	18	4	4	10	14	25	16
Venezuela	18	5	1	12	18	44	16
Chile	18	3	3	12	15	27	12

PLAY-OFF

Australia vs. **Uruguay**   1–0, 0–3

OCEANIA

The Oceania Confederation is the only one not to have at least one nation guaranteed a spot in the World Cup finals. The 10 member associations were divided into two groups of five. Each team played the other four once only. Group winners (Australia and New Zealand) then met over two legs, and the winners (Australia) advanced to a play-off against the fifth team in the South American (Uruguay) qualifying group.

OFC GROUP 1

Team	P	W	D	L	GF	GA	Pts
Australia	**4**	**4**	**0**	**0**	**66**	**0**	**12**
Fiji	4	3	0	1	27	4	9
Tonga	4	2	0	2	7	30	6
Samoa	4	1	0	3	9	18	3
American Samoa	4	0	0	4	0	57	0

PLAY-OFF

OFC GROUP 2

Team	P	W	D	L	GF	GA	Pts
New Zealand	**4**	**4**	**0**	**0**	**19**	**1**	**12**
Tahiti	4	3	0	1	14	6	9
Solomon Islands	4	2	0	2	17	10	6
Vanuatu	4	1	0	3	11	21	3
Cook Islands	4	0	0	4	2	25	0

New Zealand vs. **Australia**   0–2, 1–4

Five of FIFA's six geographical regions will be represented at the finals with Oceania the only stay-at-homes. All the previous winners of the World Cup will be present – Brazil (four titles), Germany and Italy (three each), Argentina and Uruguay (two each) plus England and France (one each) – as will four newcomers to the finals: China, Ecuador, Senegal and Slovenia.

Africa's representation is headed by Senegal, whose debut game is against France in the opening match. Making up the African quintet are Cameroon, Nigeria, South Africa and Tunisia, all of whom competed in the finals in France four years ago.

Asian fans were disappointed that only four of their nations will be present at the region's historic first hosting. Co-hosts Japan and South Korea lead the way followed by qualifiers China and Saudi Arabia. Excitement at the likely impact of travelling Chinese fans saw FIFA organize the draw so that China would play all their first-round matches in Korea.

CONCACAF, the Central and North American region, send perpetual modern qualifiers Mexico and the United States plus Costa Rica, who have not appeared in the finals since surprisingly reaching the second round in 1990. Powerful Argentina and Brazil will be the dangers from South America rather than fellow qualifiers Ecuador, Paraguay and Uruguay.

The remaining contingent of 15, almost half the competition, come from Europe headed by France. Nine other countries qualified by finishing top of their groups (Croatia, Denmark, England, Italy, Poland, Portugal, Russia, Spain and Sweden) while five (Belgium, Germany, Republic of Ireland, Slovenia and Turkey) emerged from the play-offs.

France will be last winners to benefit from direct qualification for the finals. On the eve of the draw, FIFA's Executive Committee approved a proposal from President Sepp Blatter that future winners should start their title defence in the qualifying competition.

A colourful, high-wire carnival explodes inside the Stade de France to set the 1998 World Cup finals under way.

Group A

FRANCE
Looking to repeat

World Cup Record

1930	finals 1st round	**1970**	did not qualify
1934	finals 1st round	**1974**	did not qualify
1938	quarter-final	**1978**	finals 1st round
1950	did not qualify	**1982**	fourth place
1954	finals 1st round	**1986**	third place
1958	third place	**1990**	did not qualify
1962	did not qualify	**1994**	did not qualify
1966	finals 1st round	**1998**	winners

The Coach

Roger Lemerre *Career:* Played for Sedan, Nantes, Nancy, Lens, France. Coach of Red Star Paris, Lens, Paris FC, Strasbourg, Esperance (Tunisia), Red Star Paris, French national military team.
Born: 18 June 1941 *Appointed:* August 1998

Star Performers

Fabien Barthez *Position:* Midfielder
Club: Manchester United (England) *Born:* 28 June 1971
Patrick Vieira *Position:* Midfielder
Club: Arsenal (England) *Born:* 23 June 1976
Bixente Lizarazu *Position:* Left-back
Club: Bayern Munich (Germany) *Born:* 9 December 1969
Thierry Henry *Position:* Striker
Club: Arsenal (England) *Born:* 17 August 1977
Emmanuel Petit *Position:* Midfielder
Club: Chelsea (England) *Born:* 22 September 1970

The Road to the Finals

Qualified automatically as holders

Emmanuel Petit scores the last World Cup goal of the 20th century in France's 3–0 defeat of Brazil.

France take with them to Korea and Japan an aura of invincibility born of their triumph in the Stade de France in 1998, their electrifying victory in the 2000 European Championship and their subsequent success – with a weakened team – in the Confederations Cup in Korea and Japan last year.

France will be highly favoured to become the third nation in World Cup history to win the game's greatest prize twice in succession. Italy managed the feat in 1934 and 1938, as did Brazil in 1958 and 1962. But the pressures of time, tactics and technique are such that maintaining form and inspiration over a four-year span is a trick beyond most managers and countries.

Manager Roger Lemerre may occasionally regret the lack of competitive qualifying action but his players have proved time and again that they can rise to the greatest of occasions. The 1998 World Cup triumph, secured by a 3–0 win over Brazil thanks to goals from Zinedine Zidane (two) and Manu Petit, was long overdue reward for the crucial role France had played in shaping the international game.

Robert Guerin was the first president of FIFA; Jules Rimet, also FIFA president for more than 20 years, was instrumental in creating the World Cup; and Henri Delaunay was the moving spirit behind the European Championship. On the pitch, Lucien Laurent scored the first goal in World Cup history and stars such as Raymond Kopa, Michel Platini (three times), Jean-Pierre Papin and Zidane have all been voted European Footballer of the Year, while Just Fontaine is the record goalscorer in a World Cup finals – 13 in 1958.

Zidane has also, twice, been acclaimed FIFA World Player of the Year. But he has also

THE COACH
ROGER LEMERRE

Roger Lemerre played six times in defence for France and 414 league matches before coaching Lens, Strasbourg and Esperance of Tunisia. Returned to the French Federation, guiding the military team to a world championship victory. Succeeded Aime Jacquet as senior national coach after the 1998 World Cup and led *Les Bleus* to victory at Euro 2000.

been the first to pay tribute to the team ethic which has provided France with their foundation of success – not only among the players but in the coaching staff behind the scenes at the much-admired national technical centre at Clairefontaine.

Staying together

When Italy won their double, only two players played in both the 1934 and 1938 Finals; in Brazil's case no fewer than eight players were winners in both 1958 and 1962. France will be probably much closer to the Brazil model.

At least a half of the victorious 1998 squad are likely to be defending French honour in the Far East, including goalkeeper Fabien Barthez, defenders Lilian Thuram, Marcel Desailly, Vincent Candela and Bixente Lizarazu, midfielders Petit, Patrick Vieira and Robert Pires, Zidane plus forwards Thierry Henry and David Trezeguet. In fact, 15 of the 22 who enjoyed the success in 1998 were in the 20-man squad chosen for an October 2001 friendly against Algeria.

The psychological key to retaining the World Cup could be a lack of complacency. As Aime Jacquet, who stepped down as manager after the 1998 glory ride down the

ZINEDINE ZIDANE

Position: Midfield **Club:** Real Madrid (Sp)
Previous clubs: Cannes, Bordeaux, Juventus (It)
Born: 23 June 1972
Intl apps: 70 **Intl goals:** 19

Zinedine Zidane is the world's No 1 footballer according to no less an authority than Pele. Brought up in Marseille, with an Algerian family background, Zidane represents the modern face of cosmopolitan French football. A starring role with UEFA Cup finalists Bordeaux in 1995–96 earned a transfer to Juventus and the Italian experience turned him into the two-goal match-winner when France defeated Brazil in the 1998 World Cup Final. He also inspired France to their Euro 2000 triumph. World and European player awards preceded more headlines for Zidane when he joined Real Madrid in 2001 from Juventus for a world record £45 million.

Zinedine Zidane has proved to be the man with the golden touch for France on all the big occasions, scoring twice in the World Cup Final and the Euro 2000 semi-final winner.

player. Juventus were not concerned. They had already made a down-payment on a transfer deal to take him to Turin.

Headline man

On the international scene, France did not need to qualify for the 1998 World Cup finals as they were the hosts, but the team, under Aime Jacquet, were well prepared. Against Italy in the quarter-final stage Zidane converted the first penalty of the shoot-out – after a goalless 120 minutes – as France advanced to the semi-final, 4–3. After beating Croatia 2–1 in the semi-final, Zidane and France were in the Final, at the Stade de France, St. Denis.

It was the perfect stage for Zidane, who was outstanding in *Les Bleus'* 3–0 defeat of Brazil in the Final. He scored twice, both times with headers from corners, to put the seal on a fantastic tournament.

"Zizou" was arguably even better as France became the first country ever to win the European Championship two years after claiming the World Cup. Zidane struck a stunning free-kick to put France on their way to quarter-final victory against Spain and converted the "golden goal" penalty to end Portugal's dream in the semi-final. Italy stifled Zidane in the Final, but France still won 2–1.

Celebrating his 30th birthday one day after the quarter-finals, Zidane would like nothing more than to celebrate his personal milestone a week later in the World Cup Final at Yokohama.

Champs Elysées, said: "We do not think we know it all – just because we are champions of Europe and the world."

World's best

In Zinedine Zidane, France may well have the world's best player in their World Cup finals squad. He was the subject of the largest transfer fee in football history when Real Madrid paid Juventus £45 million in summer 2001. It was a lot of money, but Zidane is a complete footballer at the peak of his career, arguably France's greatest ever player. He is a former European Footballer of the Year and a two-time World Player of the Year

Zidane was just 16 years old when he made his debut for Cannes. Four years later, he moved to Bordeaux, and in August 1994, aged 22, Zidane made his international debut against the Czech Republic. The match ended 2–2, and he scored both of France's goals.

Bordeaux reached the UEFA Cup Final in 1996, after qualifying via the Inter-Toto Cup. But when Euro 96 came around, Zidane was a peripheral figure. It turned out that he had played in more matches (57) in the season leading up to the tournament than any other

DENMARK
Can they bring home the bacon?

World Cup Record

1930	did not enter	**1970**	did not qualify
1934	did not enter	**1974**	did not qualify
1938	did not enter	**1978**	did not qualify
1950	did not enter	**1982**	did not qualify
1954	did not enter	**1986**	finals 2nd round
1958	failed to qualify	**1990**	failed to qualify
1962	did not enter	**1994**	failed to qualify
1966	did not qualify	**1998**	quarter-final

The Coach

Morten Olsen *Career:* Played for B1901 Copenhagen, Cercle Brugge (Belgium), RWDM (Belgium), Anderlecht (Belgium), FC Köln, Denmark. Coach of Brondby, Köln (Germany), Ajax (Holland).
Born: 14 August 1949 *Appointed:* July 2000

Star Performers

Thomas Sorensen *Position:* Goalkeeper
Club: Sunderland (England) *Born:* 12 June 1976
Thomas Helveg *Position:* Defender
Club: Milan (Italy) *Born:* 24 June 1971
Thomas Gravesen *Position:* Midfielder
Club: Everton (England) *Born:* 3 November 1976
Dennis Rommedahl *Position:* Striker
Club: PSV Eindhoven (Holland) *Born:* 22 July 1978
Jon Dahl Thomasson *Position:* Striker
Club: Feyenoord (Holland) *Born:* 29 August 1976

The Road to the Finals

Iceland 1–2 Denmark
Northern Ireland 1–1 Denmark
Denmark 1–1 Bulgaria
Malta 0–5 Denmark
Czech Republic 0–0 Denmark
Denmark 2–1 Czech Republic
Denmark 2–1 Malta
Denmark 1–1 Northern Ireland
Bulgaria 0–2 Denmark
Denmark 6–0 Iceland

Forward Dennis Rommedahl represents the new generation of "Danish Dynamite".

Captained by Morten Olsen, Denmark reached the European Championship semi-finals in 1984, the World Cup second round two years later and, in 1992, they astonished the world game by carrying off the European crown.

Now Olsen is heading back to the World Cup finals as national coach with the ambition of going further than the second round. That was the end of the road back in Mexico in 1986, during his playing days. At that time the Danish team revolved around the legendary Laudrup brothers, Michael and Brian.

Denmark clinched automatic qualification for the finals in Korea and Japan by thrashing Iceland 6–0 in their concluding outing in European qualifying group three. The quality of Olsen's rebuilt Danish outfit is evident from the manner in which, once they had moved to the top of the group, they refused to be shaken by the pressure exerted by pursuers from the Czech Republic and Bulgaria.

The Danes finished as they began the group, with victory over Iceland. The launch pad was a 2–1 win in Reykjavik in September 2000 when the Danes hit back from a goal down courtesy of strikes from Jon Dahl Tomasson and Morten Bisgaard. It was the ideal encouragement after Denmark had lost all their three matches at the finals of the 2000 European Championship in Holland and Belgium.

Bo Johansson, the Swedish-born coach who had steered Denmark to a narrow defeat at the hands of Brazil in the World Cup quarter-finals in France in 1998, handed command to Olsen after the Euro exit and the switch paid off. Not that it was easy. The initial win in Iceland was followed by a draw against Northern Ireland then a draw and defeat against Bulgaria which sandwiched a five-goal thrashing of Malta in which Ebbe Sand scored a hat-trick.

Turning point

The turning point, however, was the Danes' battling 2–1 home win over the Czech Republic in Copenhagen last June. Sand and Tomasson scored the goals which not only lifted the Danes in the table but provided an essential injection of confidence. In the end they finished two points clear of the Czechs and five ahead of Bulgaria. Denmark conceded a miserly six goals in their 10 games and Sand ended up as joint top scorer in the European qualifying mini-leagues with nine goals (level with Ukraine's Andriy Shevchenko).

The squad has a balanced look about it. Thomas Sorensen has taken over securely in goal from Peter Schmeichel, while vast experience and rock-solid tackling are qualities shared by defenders such as Thomas Helveg and Jan Heintze. Stig Tofting and Thomas Gravesen fire the engine in midfield with Tomasson and Sand the dangers in attack.

The challenge now is whether Olsen's men can match the achievements of the Denmark of the Laudrup brothers.

Ebbe Sand celebrates his opening goal for Denmark in their crucial 2–1 qualifying win over the Czech Republic in Copenhagen.

THE COACH

MORTEN OLSEN

Outstanding central defender and captain of Denmark at the 1986 World Cup finals. Played 102 times for his country receiving only one yellow card. Established his coaching reputation with Brondby after retiring and then set off on an international career with Koln and Ajax. Succeeded Bo Johansson as boss of Denmark after Euro 2000.

LOOK OUT FOR

EBBE SAND

Position: Striker *Club:* Schalke '04 (Germany)
Previous club: Brondby
Born: 19 July 1972 *Intl apps:* 41 *Intl goals:* 16

Ebbe Sand was a late arrival in terms of international recognition. He made his name with top domestic club Brondby and appeared destined to stay there despite appearing for Denmark in the 1998 World Cup and 2000 European Championship finals. A transfer in the summer of 1999 to German club Schalke '04 transformed his prospects. Sand finished as the Bundesliga's joint top scorer with 22 goals in the 2000–01 season. His nose for goals shot Schalke into the Champions League while another nine fired Denmark – despite missing the retired Laudrup brothers – into the World Cup finals once more.

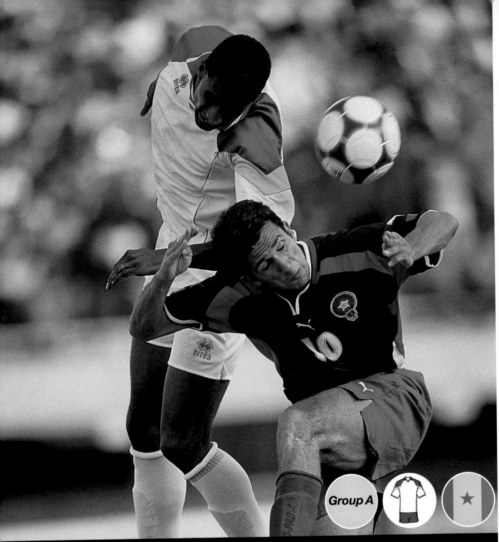

World Cup Record

1930	did not enter	1970	did not qualify
1934	did not enter	1974	did not qualify
1938	did not enter	1978	did not qualify
1950	did not enter	1982	did not qualify
1954	did not enter	1986	did not qualify
1958	did not enter	1990	did not enter
1962	did not enter	1994	did not qualify
1966	withdrew	1998	did not qualify

The Coach

Bruno Metsu *Career:* Played for Dunkerque, Lille, Nice, Anderlecht (Belgium), Valenciennes, Beauvais. Coach of Beauvais, Lille, Sedan, Guinea national team.
Born: 28 January 1954 *Appointed:* October 2000

Star Performers

Moussa N'Diaye *Position:* Midfield
Club: Sedan (France) *Born:* 31 December 1981
El-Hadji Diouf *Position:* Striker
Club: Lens (France) *Born:* 15 January 1981
Omar Daf *Position:* Defender
Club: Sochaux (France) *Born:* 12 February 1977
Ferdinand Coli *Position:* Defender
Club: Lens (France) *Born:* 10 September 1973
Tony Sylva *Position:* Goalkeeper
Club: Monaco (France) *Born:* 17 May 1975

The Road to the Finals

Benin 1–1 Senegal	Senegal 4–0 Namibia
Senegal 1–0 Benin	Senegal 3–0 Algeria
Algeria 1–1 Senegal	Egypt 1–0 Senegal
Senegal 0–0 Egypt	Senegal 1–0 Morocco
Morocco 0–0 Senegal	Namibia 0–5 Senegal

Habib Beye makes his height tell in Senegal's 1–0 qualifying win over Morocco.

Group A

SENEGAL
Africa's surprise package

Senegal have come from virtually nowhere to world status in less than two years. They are Africa's newcomers to the World Cup finals and further proof, if any were needed, of the continent's fast-developing football power.

They went into the qualifying competition having neither won the African Nations Cup nor even having reached the Final. But the signs were there for anyone who wished to take note. In the 2000 African Nations Cup, Senegal reached the quarter-finals, where they lost in extra time to co-hosts Nigeria. It says everything about fans' expectations that a squad built around French league-based players were welcomed back to Dakar by an exuberant 25,000 crowd at the airport.

They nearly did not make it past the first round of the World Cup qualifiers, beating Benin only 2–1 over two legs with goals from Mohammed N'Diaye in the away leg and Salif Ba back in Dakar. German coach Peter Schnittger burst out laughing when Senegal were then drawn against Algeria, Egypt, Morocco and Namibia in the group phase. Just about every neutral observer envisaged them finishing in around fourth place.

Stars return for new coach

Senegal made it of course, though Schnittger did not. The struggle to beat Benin drew a line under his reign and he was replaced by Frenchman Bruno Metsu, whose only previous experience in African national team football had been with Guinea. Metsu's first challenge was off the pitch, persuading several grumpy players who had refused to play for Schnittger to return to the squad.

Initial results were impressive. Senegal drew away against Algeria and Morocco and at home to Egypt. Namibia and Algeria were both beaten in Dakar, thanks to a pair of hat-tricks from El-Hadji Diouf of Lens.

Senegal went down 1-0 away to Egypt but it was their only qualifing reverse. Diouf scored the lone goal which beat Morocco – who had needed only a draw to qualify – and then another in the 5–0 victory away to Namibia which sent Senegal to the finals for the first time. That was the most tense day in the country's football history since Senegal needed to win well and rely on Egypt not winning in Algeria – it ended 1–1.

Senegal's qualifying record was five wins and four draws in 10 matches, scoring 16 goals and conceding only three. Diouf, with eight goals, was top scorer.

Virtually all the members of Senegal's line-up were drawn from the French championship, with Morocco-based goalkeeper Omar Diallo from Khouribga being the only "outsider".

Reaction to qualification was so fervent that State President Abdoulaye Wade cut short a state visit to Europe to fly home to welcome the squad back. He presented each player with one of the country's highest honours – the National Order of the Lion – to encourage them to roar all the more loudly in the finals.

Group A

URUGUAY
Back where they belong

Uruguay were the last nation to claim a place in the 2002 finals after beating Australia 3–1 on aggregate in a play-off. Despite their small size and meagre financial resources, fans expect Uruguay – the first hosts and first winners – to punch above their weight at the World Cup.

Coach Victor Pua's men had been forced to go the extra length of facing the Oceania section winners – a 14,500-mile round-trip – because they finished fifth in the South American qualifying group. Yet even that could be considered a success given the turbulent background to the Uruguayans' campaign.

Former Argentina boss Daniel Passarella had been brought in to turn results around but he quit in the spring of 2001 after squabbling with top clubs Penarol and Nacional over player release. Simultaneously the domestic game was rocked by a bribes scandal and star playmaker Alvaro Recoba became embroiled, in Italy, in a forged passport controversy.

By mid-2001 it had become clear that Uruguay's best qualifying hope lay in the play-off route. A 1–0 home win over Brazil edged them ahead of Colombia into fifth place and they clung on by the narrowest possible margin.

They drew 1–1 at home to Argentina in their last game while Colombia, simultaneously, pulled level on points courtesy of a 4–0 win away to already-qualified Paraguay. But Colombia had needed a five-goal margin and the Celeste (Light Blues) secured the play-off on goal difference by virtue of a single goal.

Global challenge

Six days later, Uruguay were in Melbourne where they lost 1–0 to Australia. Five days on from that, they were turning the tables 3–0 in Montevideo. Malaga's Dario Silva, barely recovered from a collarbone fracture suffered against Argentina, struck the first goal. Substitute Richard Morales grabbed the other two.

Pua, former national team midfielder and then national youth coach, was immediately rewarded with the extension of his contract up to the finals. Players such as the Juventus trio of goalkeeper Fabian Carini, central defender Paolo Montero and midfielder Fabian O'Neil provide him with a solid foundation along with the likes of the highly-talented Recoba and striker Silva.

Uruguay dominated world football in the first half of the century, winning the World Cup both in 1930 and 1950. Jose Nasazzi, Hector Scarone, Obdulio Varela and Juan Schiaffino are considered among the greatest players ever to emerge from South America. But financial problems have undermined Uruguayan teams' ability to compete on the world stage and the finest players are lured abroad as soon as they have established anything approaching a reputation.

Pua says: "This works two ways. It is hard for us to bring our stars back for big matches and then they play at a very different level to our home-based players. At least now we have time to integrate everyone into our plans for the World Cup."

World Cup Record

1930	winners	**1970**	fourth place
1934	did not enter	**1974**	finals 1st round
1938	did not enter	**1978**	did not qualify
1950	winners	**1982**	did not qualify
1954	fourth place	**1986**	finals 1st round
1958	did not qualify	**1990**	finals 2nd round
1962	finals 1st round	**1994**	did not qualify
1966	quarter-finals	**1998**	did not qualify

The Coach

Victor Pua *Career:* Played for Nacional, Sevilla (Spain) Uruguay. Coach of River Plate, Montevideo, Uruguay yth. *Born:* 31 March 1956 *Appointed:* February 2001

Star Performers

Dario Silva *Position:* Striker
Club: Malaga (Spain) *Born:* 2 November 1972
Paolo Montero *Position:* Defender
Club: Juventus (Italy) *Born:* 15 August 1976
Alvaro Recoba *Position:* Striker
Club: Internazionale (Italy) *Born:* 3 September 1971
Fabian Carini *Position:* Goalkeeper
Club: Juventus (Italy) *Born:* 26 December 1979
Walter Pandiani *Position:* Striker
Club: Deportivo La Coruña (Spain) *Born:* 27 April 1970

The Road to the Finals

Uruguay 1–0 Bolivia	Uruguay 0–1 Paraguay
Paraguay 1–0 Uruguay	Chile 0–1 Uruguay
Uruguay 2–1 Chile	Uruguay 1–0 Brazil
Brazil 1–1 Uruguay	Venezuela 2–0 Uruguay
Uruguay 3–1 Venezuela	Peru 0–2 Uruguay
Uruguay 0–0 Peru	Uruguay 1–1 Colombia
Colombia 1–0 Uruguay	Ecuador 1–1 Uruguay
Uruguay 4–0 Ecuador	Uruguay 1–1 Argentina
Argentina 2–1 Uruguay	Australia 1–0 Uruguay
Bolivia 0–0 Uruguay	Uruguay 3–0 Australia

Alvaro Recoba (20) outwits Australia's Josip Skoko in Uruguay's play-off triumph.

27

Interestingly, Spain did not rely on one single player – even Real Madrid's Raul – in attack. Their 21 goals were shared among no fewer than 11 players, with Raul top-scoring on "only" four and playmaker Gaixka Mendieta and veteran centre-back Fernando Hierro collecting three apiece.

The message is that Spain can score goals from any position – including defence and midfield – and also boast a variety of attacking options. Raul may have any one of a handful of outstanding partners including club-mate Fernando Morientes, Milan's Javi Moreno and Deportivo La Coruna's Diego Tristan.

But Spain will bring to Korea and Japan more than the sum total of demonstrable experience. Iker Casillas is one of the finest young goalkeepers in the world and keeps Santiago Canizares on his toes. In attack, a great future is predicted for the Atletico Madrid teenager Fernando Torres if Camacho dare gamble on his boy wonder's thrilling potential.

Group B

SPAIN
Maybe this will be the year

Spain boasts some of the world's greatest clubs, finest stadia and most fanatical fans. It is long overdue time for the national team to match that status. Coached by Jose Camacho and inspired in attack by Raul, Spain are promising to relegate to history their painful reputation as a team who punch below their weight at the World Cup.

The strange truth is that Spain's best finish was fourth back in the 1950 finals in Brazil. Since then they have either failed to qualify or flattered to deceive – even as hosts in 1982.

Outstanding managers such as Helenio Herrera, Jose Villalonga, Jose Santamaria, Luis Suarez and Javier Clemente have all found it impossible to turn the varied talents of Real Madrid, Barcelona, Valencia and Bilbao into a cohesive winning unit.

Spain did lift the European Championship in 1964 and finished runners-up in 1984. But, mostly, at top level nerves have always got the better of them – even at the last European finals when they crashed out to France in the last eight after Raul missed a last-minute penalty.

Of course, the big clubs hold responsibility for Spain's intimidating reputation. Madrid have won the European Cup a record eight times and Barcelona, Atletico Madrid, Valencia and Zaragoza have all carried off European trophies of their own from time to time. But their success has been founded largely thanks to great foreign signings and Spain's own home-grown talent has suffered a long-running and apparently incurable inferiority complex.

Camacho leads the way

Camacho, another old hero of Real Madrid and a stalwart of Spain's defence at the 1982 World Cup, intends to change all that. Initial signs are promising. Spain dominated qualifying group seven. Admittedly it was perhaps the easiest of the European mini-leagues but the Spaniards have slipped up against enough so-called minnows in the past to have learned to take nothing for granted. In the end they went through their eight-game programme unbeaten, winning six matches and drawing two, conceding only four goals and finishing way out in front.

World Cup Record

1930	did not enter	**1970**	did not qualify
1934	finals 2nd round	**1974**	did not qualify
1938	entry refused	**1978**	finals 1st round
1950	fourth place	**1982**	finals 2nd round
1954	did not qualify	**1986**	quarter-final
1958	did not qualify	**1990**	finals 2nd round
1962	finals 1st round	**1994**	quarter-final
1966	finals 1st round	**1998**	finals 1st round

The Coach

Jose Camacho
Career: Played for Real Madrid, Spain. Coach of Rayo Vallecano, Espanyol, Sevilla, Espanyol.
Born: 8 June 1955 *Appointed:* September 1998

Star Performers

Fernando Morientes *Position:* Striker
Club: Real Madrid *Born:* 5 April 1976
Fernando Hierro *Position:* Defender
Club: Real Madrid *Born:* 23 March 1968
Gaizka Mendieta *Position:* Midfielder
Club: Lazio (Italy) *Born:* 27 March 1974
Jose Cañizares *Position:* Goalkeeper
Club: Valencia *Born:* 18 December 1969
Luis Enrique *Position:* Midfielder
Club: Barcelona *Born:* 8 May 1970

The Road to the Finals

Bosnia-Herzegovina 1–2 Spain
Spain 2–0 Israel
Austria 1–1 Spain
Spain 5–0 Liechtenstein
Spain 4–1 Bosnia-Herzegovina
Israel 1–1 Spain
Spain 4–0 Austria
Liechtenstein 0–2 Spain

Fernando Morientes (9) beats Marcel Desailly of France to a cross during Spain's 2–1 victory in last year's friendly.

RAUL

(Full name: Raul Gonzalez Blanco)

Position: Forward *Club:* Real Madrid
Previous clubs: None
Born: 27 June 1977 *Intl apps:* 48 *Intl goals:* 23

Raul was the subject of one of Spanish football's biggest blunders – joining Real Madrid after cross-city neighbours Atletico scrapped the youth team in which he played. He proved such a sensation his new club were swiftly dubbed "Raul Madrid". He was fast-tracked to stardom with club and country, crowned league top scorer, won the European Champions League twice in three years and raced up to third in Madrid's all-time European Cup scoring charts, behind the legendary Alfredo Di Stefano and Ferenc Puskas. His World Cup ambition is enhanced by the memory of a decisive missed penalty in a Euro 2000 quarter-final defeat by France.

Raul, having won everything at club level with Real Madrid, has set his sights on national team targets, especially the World Cup.

THE COACH

JOSE ANTONIO CAMACHO

Camacho was a rock at the heart of Real Madrid's defence in the 1970s and 1980s when he helped them to win nine league titles. Also played 81 times for Spain, including the 1982 World Cup as hosts. Earned an equally rock-like reputation as a coach with Rayo Vallecano, Espanyol and Sevilla. Succeeded Javier Clemente as national coach.

After first round exits in 1930, 1950 and 1958, Paraguay qualified for the finals again in 1986. Led by playmaker Julio Cesar Romero – better known as Romerito, South America's Player of the Year in 1985 – they reached the second round before losing 3–0 to England in Mexico City.

The second round was the finishing post again in 1998. Amid the later euphoria which engulfed France's ultimate triumph it was largely forgotten that the hosts squeezed past the Paraguayans thanks only to a 112th-minute golden goal from captain and centre-half Laurent Blanc.

Bumpy path to the finals

Memories of that bitter defeat fired Paraguay's qualifying bid this time around. Defeat in Peru was a bad start but Chilavert

World Cup Record

1930	finals 1st round	**1970**	did not qualify
1934	did not enter	**1974**	did not qualify
1938	did not enter	**1978**	did not qualify
1950	finals 1st round	**1982**	did not qualify
1954	did not qualify	**1986**	finals 2nd round
1958	finals 1st round	**1990**	did not qualify
1962	did not qualify	**1994**	did not qualify
1966	did not qualify	**1998**	finals 2nd round

The Coach

Cesare Maldini
Career: Played for AC Milan (Italy), Italy.
Coached AC Milan (Italy), Italy Under-21, Italian national team.
Born: 1 November 1941 *Appointed:* December 2001

Star Performers

Carlos Gamarra *Position:* Central defender
Club: AEK Athens (Greece) *Born:* 17 February 1971
Roberto Acuna *Position:* Midfield
Club: Real Zaragoza (Spain) *Born:* 25 March 1972
Virgilio Ferreira *Position:* Midfielder
Club: Cerro Porteño *Born:* 23 January 1973
Jose Cardozo *Position:* Striker
Club: Toluca (Mexico) *Born:* 19 March 1971
Francisco Javier Arce *Position:* Defender
Club: Palmeiras (Brazil) *Born:* 2 April 1971

Group B

PARAGUAY
More than a one-man team

Paraguay qualified for the 2002 finals sitting in their hotel in San Cristóbal, Venezuela. Other teams' failure to win, a day before the Paraguayans were due to meet Venezuela, meant that qualification as the second, third or fourth team in the tortuous CONMEBOL qualification group was confirmed.

Paraguay go to Korea and Japan for the second successive finals intending to prove they have more to offer than one of the world game's most idiosyncratic and charismatic players. Jose Luis Chilavert is the penalty-firing, free-kick-blasting last line of defence who wants desperately to become the first goalkeeper to score a goal at the opposite

end in the World Cup's closing stages.

His prospects of achieving his dream appeared faint when Paraguay began their qualifying campaign with a 2–0 defeat in Peru. Within a year, however, Chilavert and his team-mates had got their act together, tucked themselves in behind group leaders Argentina and secured their ticket to the finals. Paraguayan fans accept that they are not the greatest power in South America. But they have won the South American Championship – the Copa America – twice, in 1953 and 1979, and will be attending the World Cup finals for the sixth time. In addition, the capital city, Asuncion, hosts the headquarters of the South American confederation, CONMEBOL.

The Road to the Finals

Peru 2–0 Paraguay	Paraguay 5–1 Peru
Paraguay 1–0 Uruguay	Uruguay 0–1 Paraguay
Paraguay 3–1 Ecuador	Ecuador 2–1 Paraguay
Chile 3–1 Paraguay	Paraguay 1–0 Chile
Paraguay 2–1 Brazil	Brazil 2–0 Paraguay
Bolivia 0–0 Paraguay	Paraguay 5–1 Bolivia
Argentina 1–1 Paraguay	Paraguay 2–2 Argentina
Paraguay 3–0 Venezuela	Venezuela 3–1 Paraguay
Colombia 0–2 Paraguay	Paraguay 0–4 Colombia

Nelson Cuevas lets fly at goal as Paraguay step up the pressure on fellow qualifiers Ecuador during a 2–1 defeat in Quito.

JOSE LUIS CHILAVERT

Position: Goalkeeper   *Club:* Strasbourg (Fr)
Previous clubs: Nacional, Velez Sarsfield (Arg)
Born: 27 July 1965   *Intl apps:* 50
Intl goals: 6

Jose Luis Chilavert, one of the world's most charismatic goalkeepers, has scored more than 50 goals from penalties and free-kicks. His remaining ambition is to become the first goalkeeper to score in the opposition's net in the World Cup finals. His chances will be restricted because of a two-game suspension which he brings to the finals after being sent off in the qualifying competition. Chilavert's career has been marked by angry squabbles with coaches, journalists, politicians and team-mates. When playing in Argentine club football he was twice flattened by fireworks thrown from the crowd by hooligan fans of rival teams.

Goalkeeper Jose Luis Chilavert celebrates another massive step forward for Paraguayan football.

and company revived with successive victories over Uruguay and Ecuador, 1–0 and 3–1, respectively.

Defeat in Chile was then forgotten in the excitement generated by a 2–1 victory over Brazil. Goals from Carlos Paredes and Jorge Campos secured a victory after which the Paraguayans never looked back. They even forced a goalless draw away to the rampant Argentines and then won 2–0 away to Colombia – with Chilavert thumping home the second goal in the last minute.

The former South American Footballer of the Year fired another goal, from the penalty spot, in the subsequent 5–1 home win over Peru. All that remains for him now is a repeat performance in the finals themselves.

Unfortunately for him and Paraguay, Chilavert will have to sit out the first two games of the finals as he completes a four-match suspension picked up during the qualifying tournament.

THE COACH

CESARE MALDINI

Maldini was sweeper and captain when AC Milan became the first Italian club to win the European Champions Cup in 1963. As you coach, he then helped launch the career of son Paolo. Maldini senior guided Italy to the 1998 World Cup quarter-finals. Appointed by Paraguay in December in place of sacked Sergio Markarian.

Group B

They were given little chance against Romania, especially after winning only 2–1 at home. But in Bucharest Mladen Rudonja chose the perfect moment for his first goal in 50 internationals. Cosmin Contra equalised and Romania struck the bar and had shots cleared off the line but all to no avail. Slovenia were through to the World Cup finals for the first time.

Srecko Katanec is one of the hottest young coaches in the world game. He starred as a wing-half or midfielder with Partizan Belgrade and then in Italy with Sampdoria under veteran Vujadin Boskov before turning to coaching himself.

Katanec insists that "team spirit is what matters the most" and players such as goalkeeper Marko Simeunovic, defender Marinko Galic, midfielders Ales Ceh and Dzoni Novak live up to that motto. Zahovic is a different matter – but that is what makes Slovenia such dangerously unpredictable opponents.

SLOVENIA
Continuing to surprise

Slovenia and "surprise" are words which go together after the latest remarkable exploit of one of European football's newest nations. In a few short years Slovenia have raced from nowhere to a place among the elite not merely in Europe but in the world.

It was little more than a decade ago that Slovenia emerged as an independent state from the wreckage of the former Yugoslavia. The national championship was launched in the autumn of 1991 and Slovenia's clubs stepped out into European competition a year later. The national team entered the European Championship qualifying process in the autumn of 1994.

They won only three matches in the Euro 96 qualifying series and finished next to bottom of their group. The 1998 World Cup qualifiers were much worse: Slovenia lost seven of their eight matches and finished bottom of the group.

Their graduation to the Euro 2000 finals was thus a football miracle – but it was

nothing compared with events in Belgium and Holland. Viewed as naïve minnows, Slovenia drew 3–3 with Yugoslavia – after leading astonishingly by 3–0 – lost 2–1 to Spain and drew 0–0 with Norway. Zlatko Zahovic was among the finest forwards on view.

Could lightning strike twice? The prospects appeared slim when they opened their World Cup campaign with a 2–2 draw in the Faroe Islands, a win in Luxembourg and a home draw against Switzerland. Russia were racing away at the top of group one and the runners-up spot appeared to lie between the Swiss and Yugoslavia.

Staying alive

Zahovic kept Slovenia's hopes alive with an injury-time equaliser against Yugoslavia. Then he scored both goals in a 2–0 home win over Luxembourg and Sebastjan Cimirotic struck the winner in Switzerland. Slovenia remained unbeaten, handed Russia its only qualifying defeat and clung on to earn a play-off against Romania with a 3–0 win against the Faroe Islands in Ljubljana.

World Cup Record

1930	did not enter	**1970**	did not enter
1934	did not enter	**1974**	did not enter
1938	did not enter	**1978**	did not enter
1950	did not enter	**1982**	did not enter
1954	did not enter	**1986**	did not enter
1958	did not enter	**1990**	did not enter
1962	did not enter	**1994**	did not enter
1966	did not enter	**1998**	did not qualify

The Coach

Srecko Katanec *Career:* Played for Ljubljana, Olimpija, Partizan Belgrade (Yugoslavia), Stuttgart (Germany), Sampdoria (Italy), Yugoslavia national team, Slovenia national team. Coach of Slovenia Under-21 team, HIT Gorica. *Born:* 16 July 1963 *Appointed:* July 1998

Star Performers

Zlatko Zahovic *Position:* Striker *Club:* Benfica (Portugal) *Born:* 1 February 1971
Milan Osterc *Position:* Striker *Club:* Hapoel Tel Aviv (Israel) *Born:* 4 July 1975
Marko Simeunovic *Position:* Goalkeeper *Club:* Maribor *Born:* 6 December 1967
Marinko Galic *Position:* Defender *Club:* Rudar Velenje *Born:* 22 April 1970
Mladen Rudonja *Position:* Striker *Club:* Portsmouth (England) *Born:* 26 July 1971

The Road to the Finals

Faroe Islands 2–2 Slovenia	Switzerland 0–1 Slovenia
Luxembourg 1–2 Slovenia	Slovenia 2–1 Russia
Slovenia 2–2 Switzerland	Yugoslavia 1–1 Slovenia
Russia 1–1 Slovenia	Slovenia 3–0 Faroe Islands
Slovenia 1–1 Yugoslavia	Slovenia 2–1 Romania
Slovenia 2–0 Luxembourg	Romania 1–1 Slovenia

Zoran Pavlovic flies the flag after defeating Romania to lift Slovenia into the World Cup finals for the first time.

Group B

SOUTH AFRICA
A chance to advance

World Cup Record

1930 did not enter	1970 did not enter
1934 did not enter	1974 did not enter
1938 did not enter	1978 did not enter
1950 did not enter	1982 did not enter
1954 did not enter	1986 did not enter
1958 did not enter	1990 did not enter
1962 did not enter	1994 did not qualify
1966 suspended	1998 finals 1st round

The Coach

Carlos Queiroz
Career: Coach of Portugal youth, Portugal, Sporting Lisbon (Portugal), Nagoya Grampus Eight (Japan), New York/New Jersey MetroStars (USA), United Arab Emirates.
Born: 1 March 1953 *Appointed:* September 2000

Star Performers

Shaun Bartlett *Position:* Striker
Club: Charlton Athletic (England) *Born:* 31 October 1972
Pierre Issa *Position:* Defender
Club: Watford (England) *Born:* 11 August 1975
Sisbusiso Zuma *Position:* Midfield
Club: FC Copenhagen (Denmark) *Born:* 23 June 1975
Hans Vonk *Position:* Goalkeeper
Club: Heerenveen (Holland) *Born:* 30 January 1970
Quinton Fortune *Position:* Midfield
Club: Manchester United (England) *Born:* 21 May 1977

The Road to the Finals

Lesotho 0–2 South Africa
South Africa 1–0 Lesotho
Zimbabwe 0–2 South Africa
South Africa 1–0 Burkina Faso
Malawi 1–2 South Africa
South Africa 2–1 Zimbabwe
Burkina Faso 1–1 South Africa
South Africa 2–0 Malawi

Shaun Bartlett keeps everything under control as South Africa reach the finals for the second successive time.

South Africa raced from international isolation to pace-setters in a decade. The end of apartheid prompted their readmission to FIFA and the springboard to victory as hosts in the 1996 African Nations Cup and a first-ever qualification for the World Cup finals two years later.

South Africa were led to the 2002 finals by a man who knows all about World Cups, albeit at youth level. Portuguese boss Carlos Queiroz is one of the most respected coaches in the international game and contracting him in mid-2000 was a major coup for SAFA.

South Africa's national team, under a succession of coaches, had remained faithful to a 3-5-2 tactical shape. Queiroz, however, preferred the Portuguese model 4-4-2 with which he took Bafana Bafana (The Boys) safely through to the 2002 finals despite the long-term absence of veteran central defender Lucas Radebe.

Queiroz used 37 players in taking South Africa through from their opening match in Lesotho when a goal from record marksman Shaun Bartlett set them on a 2–0 winning way. Bartlett also scored the only goal in the return to send South Africa into the group phase.

The draw was kind to Queiros and Co, matching them with Burkina Faso, Malawi, Zimbabwe and Guinea. After three rounds of matches Guinea withdrew through lack of funds and their results were expunged.

Tragedy follows misfortune

The Guinea problem was overshadowed, however, by tragic events when South Africa visited Zimbabwe in Harare. The South Africans were 2–0 ahead when a tear gas assault by panicking policemen provoked a stampede which left 13 fans dead.

It was the first in a series of crowd disasters in Africa – including South Africa – which raised serious questions about management of the game across the continent. Security and crowd control had to be stepped up as South Africa's footballers sought to maintain their steady progress towards Korea and Japan.

In the event they qualified both unbeaten and with a game to spare. A 1–1 draw in Burkina Faso in the penultimate round was sufficient with FC Kobenhavn's Sisbusiso Zuma scoring the all-important goal. Charlton striker Bartlett finished as South Africa's top marksman in qualifying with four goals.

Bartlett was also South Africa's top scorer at the 1998 finals in France, albeit with only two goals, scored in the 2–2 draw with Saudi Arabia with which the South Africans wound up their programme after a 3–0 defeat by hosts France and a 1–1 draw with Denmark.

In the wake of South Africa losing out to Germany for hosting rights in 2006, FIFA intimated that Africa will be the venue in 2010. As South Africa boasts more than one million registered footballers and the richest professional league in Africa, their prospects of earning those host rights would clearly be enhanced by progress beyond the first round in Korea and Japan.

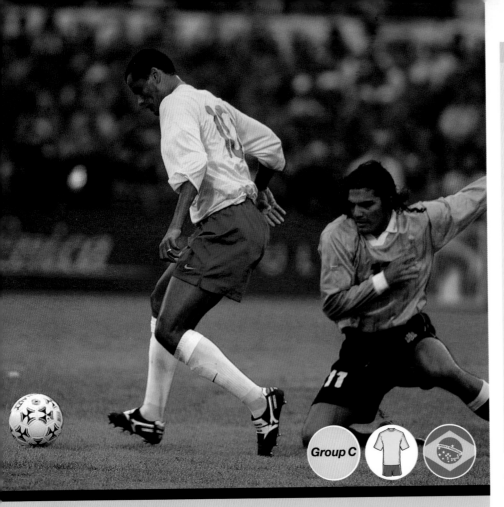

Group C

RIVALDO

(Full name: Vitor Borba Ferreira)

Position: Forward *Club:* Barcelona (Sp)
Previous clubs: Mogi-Mirim, Corinthians, Palmeiras, Deportivo La Coruna (Sp)
Born: 19 April 1972 *Intl apps:* 40 *Intl goals:* 15

Rivaldo, former World Player of the Year and European Footballer of the Year, has earned more admirers in Europe than in Brazil. Back home, he is an ongoing subject of controversy but in Europe he is accepted as one of the finest footballers in the world. He has the ability to drift in from the left and score or create a host of goals for Spain's Barcelona. Rivaldo cost the Catalan club £16 million when he was signed to replace Inter-bound Ronaldo. He emerged the winner of a notorious run-in at Barcelona with coach Louis Van Gaal after Rivaldo objected to being played out of position.

Rivaldo turns Uruguay's Federico Magallanes inside out in one of Brazil's brighter moments on the World Cup 2002 qualifying trail.

BRAZIL

For once an unknown quantity

Brazil have competed in every World Cup finals since the inaugural event in Uruguay in 1930. It is a proud, unique record but one which appeared under threat as they staggered through the 2002 qualifying tournament, securing their ticket for the finals on the last matchday when they defeated minnows Venezuela 3–0.

The Brazilians, record four-times winners of football's greatest prize and home of some

THE COACH

LUIZ FELIPE SCOLARI

"Big Phil" was Brazil's third coach in the qualifying tournament after short-lived reigns of Wanderley Luxemburgo and Emerson Leao. Had won the South American Copa Libertadores with Gremio in 1995 and Palmeiras in 1999. Had a later spell with Gremio and also coached Criciuma and Cruzeiro – whom he quit for the Brazil job.

of the game's greatest players down the years, lost six times in the preliminary group. They also changed coaches on three occasions.

Two goals from Luizao and another from World Player of the Year Rivaldo against Venezuela in Sao Luiz prompted an almost audible sigh of relief the length and breadth of a nation which lives and breathes football like no other. Yet the fact that Brazil stuttered in qualifying will not affect their status among the favourites to win in South Korea and Japan.

Brazil can boast that they are the only nation to have won on the 'wrong' continent – courtesy of their initial triumph in Sweden in 1958. That was the start of a 12-year run in which Brazil completed the hat-trick with victories in Chile in 1962 and then in Mexico in 1970. They carried off their fourth Cup in the United States in 1994 and were runners-up in 1998.

Qualifying traumas

Brazil began the tortuous qualifying campaign well enough, with a goalless draw

away to Colombia and victories over Ecuador (3–2) and Peru (1–0 away). Defeats in Paraguay and Chile came either side of a 3–1 home success over Argentina.

At that point Brazil boss Wanderley Luxemburgo took his younger players off to the Olympic Games in Sydney, which is when the wheels came off. Failure to win the one international title which eludes Brazil led to Luxemburgo's dismissal on the return to Rio de Janeiro.

New boss Emerson Leao upset the team balance by changing tactics and bringing in new players. He lasted only as long as a defeat in Ecuador and a home draw against Peru. Thus former Cruizero boss Luiz Felipe Scolari had to complete the job. He had an inauspicious start with a quarter-final exit in the Copa America and a qualifying defeat in Uruguay. Home wins over Paraguay 2–0 and Chile 2–0 put Brazil on the brink of qualifying, but it was delayed by a 3–1 loss in the high altitude conditions of La Paz, Bolivia.

No-one doubts Brazil's talent. The challenge is in harnessing that ability and sorting out the political balance between the superstars based in Rio, Sao Paulo and Europe. Defensively Cafu and Roberto Carlos remain among the world's finest full-backs but, in attack, Barcelona's Rivaldo is unpopular with Brazil's fans and no-one knows whether Internazionale's Ronaldo will be fit.

For once, no-one knows what to expect of Brazil at the World Cup finals.

World Cup Record

1930	finals 1st round	**1970**	champions
1934	finals 1st round	**1974**	4th place
1938	third place	**1978**	third place
1950	runners-up	**1982**	finals 2nd round
1954	quarter-finals	**1986**	quarter-finals
1958	champions	**1990**	finals 2nd round
1962	champions	**1994**	champions
1966	finals 1st round	**1998**	runners-up

The Coach

Luiz Felipe Scolari
Career: Coach of Palmeiras, Criciuma,
Cruzeiro
Born: 1 September 1948 *Appointed:* June 2001

Star Performers

Vampeta *Position:* Midfielder
Club: Flamengo *Born:* 13 March 1974
Roberto Carlos *Position:* Left-back
Club: Real Madrid (Spain) *Born:* 10 April 1973
Cafu *Position:* Defender
Club: Roma (Italy) *Born:* 7 June 1970
Ronaldo *Position:* Striker
Club: Internazionale (Italy) *Born:* 22 September 1976
Denilson *Position:* Midfield
Club: Real Betis (Spain) *Born:* 24 August 1977

The Road to the Finals

Colombia 0–0 Brazil	Brazil 1–0 Colombia
Brazil 3–2 Ecuador	Ecuador 1–0 Brazil
Peru 0–1 Brazil	Brazil 1–1 Peru
Brazil 1–1 Uruguay	Uruguay 1–0 Brazil
Paraguay 2–1 Brazil	Brazil 2–0 Paraguay
Brazil 3–1 Argentina	Argentina 2–1 Brazil
Chile 3–0 Brazil	Brazil 2–0 Chile
Brazil 5–0 Bolivia	Bolivia 3–1 Brazil
Venezuela 0–6 Brazil	Brazil 3–0 Venezuela

*Cafu will provide attacking options for Brazil as either a
wing-back or full-back for a third World Cup finals.*

Group C

The Coach

Senol Gunes *Career:* Played for Trabzonspor; Coach of Trabzonspor, Boluspor, Antalyaspor, Sakaryaspor. *Born:* 1 June 1952 *Appointed:* July 2000

Star Performers

Emre Belozoglu *Position:* Midfield
Club: Internazionale (Italy) *Born:* 7 September 1980
Okan Buruk *Position:* Midfield
Club: Internazionale (Italy) *Born:* 19 October 1973
Kerimoglu Tugay *Position:* Midfield
Club: Blackburn Rovers (England) *Born:* 29 July 1975
Abdullah Ercan *Position:* Defender
Club: Fenerbahce *Born:* 8 December 1971
Recber Rustu *Position:* Goalkeeper
Club: Fenerbahce *Born:* 10 May 1973

The Road to the Finals

Turkey 2–0 Moldova	Turkey 3–3 Macedonia FYR
Sweden 1–1 Turkey	Slovakia 0–1 Turkey
Azerbaijan 0–1 Turkey	Turkey 1–2 Sweden
Turkey 1–1 Slovakia	Moldova 0–3 Turkey
Macedonia FYR 1–2 Turkey	Austria 0–1 Turkey
Turkey 3–0 Azerbaijan	Turkey 5–0 Austria

Hasan Sas (11) keeps his eyes on the ball during Turkey's 5–0 playoff thrashing of Austria in November last year.

TURKEY
Must not be underestimated

Turkish football offers one of the great success stories in the modern European game. Until the mid-1990s they were considered also-rans in international tournaments. Then, suddenly, it all changed at both club and national team level.

Football was first played in the early years of the century when Western team sports were felt undesirable. A change in the climate of opinion saw the creation of the three Istanbul clubs which still dominate Turkish football: Galatasaray, Besiktas and Fenerbahce.

THE COACH
SENOL GUNES

Senol is one of the very few former international goalkeepers to emerge later as a successful coach. Played most of his career with Trabzonspor with whom he also had two spells as coach – in between Boluspor, Antalyaspor and Sakaryaspor. Appointed national coach after Mustafa Denizli took Turkey to the quarter-finals of Euro 2000.

Turkey have reached the World Cup finals only once before, in 1954. Then, after a play-off against Spain in Rome ended all-square, a blind boy, drawing lots, pulled their name out of the hat. A 7–0 victory over South Korea was not enough to see them advance – eventual winners Germany going into the quarter-finals after a first round play-off. Turkey's stars of the era were goalkeeper Turgay and winger Kucukandonyadis Lefter.

They remained the two most famous Turkish footballers until the recent exploits of Hakan Sukur and his present team-mates. Hakan's goals fired Turkey to the finals of the 1996 European Championship in England. They were eliminated in the first round but they did not disgrace themselves against Portugal, Denmark and Croatia. As coach Fatih Terim, insisted: "What is important is getting to the finals. This will do wonders for our players' confidence."

He was right. Galatasaray became the first Turkish club to win a European trophy when they defeated Arsenal in a penalty shootout in Copenhagen to land the UEFA Cup in 2000. A few weeks later the Turkish national

team reached the European Championship quarter-finals in Belgium and Holland.

Those achievements wiped away the perception of Turkish players and teams as bad travellers, especially as to reach the knock-out stages they had defeated Belgium in Brussels. They also persuaded top clubs in Italy, England and Germany to start investing seriously in Turkish players.

Road warriors

Mustafa Denizli's men started strongly in qualifying group four. They beat Moldova, drew 1–1 away to toughest rivals Sweden and won in Azerbaijan. By the summer of 2001 they were virtually sure of a spot in the top two.

Five days in September decided first and second places. Turkey defeated Slovakia away in Bratislava to move within two points of Sweden before their second meeting, in Istanbul. The penultimate match for both teams went the visitors' way, so Turkey went into the play-offs against Austria.

Turkey were the only European nation in the play-offs to win their opening leg away from home. A goal from Internazionale Milan's Okan Buruk earned a 1–0 victory in Vienna and he scored again in the return when the Turks triumphed 5–0 to wrap up a 6–0 aggregate success. Hakan, as ever, was also among the marksmen.

At international level Turkey had earned the right to be considered premier league regulars.

Group C

CHINA
Wanting to make a good impression

China's debut in the World Cup finals may prove the most significant feature of the 2002 World Cup. The world game has long waited for Asian football's sleeping giant to awaken. Qualification came just weeks after Beijing won hosting rights to the 2008 Olympic Games – two events which may tip the balance of world sport.

China took part in the first international game played on Asian soil, against the Philippines, in Manila, in February 1913, in the Far Eastern Games. However, politics regarding neighbours meant China was excluded from international tournaments for many years. When the national team did compete, its players and tactics were revealed as naïve.

Once the domestic game had been reorganized into a recognisable club and league structure, China's national team moved forward. They should have reached the World Cup finals in 1998 but missed out after a home defeat by already-eliminated Qatar in the final round. Determination not to slip up again persuaded the federation to appoint the most famously talismanic manager in World Cup history: Bora Milutinovic.

Been there, done that ...

He had set a record by managing four different nations at the finals: hosts Mexico in 1986, Costa Rica (1990), hosts United States (1994) and Nigeria (1998). Each nation reached the second round. But the Serb had never overseen a nation through a complete qualifying campaign – until he took up the China challenge, a run of 14 matches in 180 days.

Milutinovic brought China comfortably through the first stage in which they crushed the Maldives – winning 10–1 at home – Cambodia and Indonesia. In the final round group stage, midfielder Li Xiao Peng set them on their way to a 3–0 win over the United Arab Emirates and China followed up with two victories over Oman, a 1–1 draw in Qatar and 2–0 home win over Uzbekistan. Qi

Hong's solitary goal against the UAE was enough to ensure qualification as group winners with two matches to go.

It was not always fun to watch. Milutinovic drilled his team into a style more pragmatic than pretty, built around giant goalkeeper Jiang Jin, British-based central defender Fan Zhiyi, midfield workers Li Tie and Li Xiao and German-trained strikers Yang Chen (Eintracht Frankfurt) and top-scoring Xie Hui (Kickers Offenbach).

By the time China go to the World Cup finals it is likely that Sun Jihai will have slotted back into his defensive duties after being suspended for a year by FIFA, the world governing body, for attacking a referee during the last Olympic Games qualifying tournament.

Whether Milutinovic would still be in charge appeared the subject of some doubt after the qualifying competition when the Chinese media suggested that Shen Xianfu, who took China to the second round of last year's World Youth Cup, might be promoted.

World Cup Record

1930 did not enter	**1970** did not enter
1934 did not enter	**1974** did not enter
1938 did not enter	**1978** did not enter
1950 did not enter	**1982** did not qualify
1954 did not enter	**1986** did not qualify
1958 did not qualify	**1990** did not qualify
1962 did not enter	**1994** did not qualify
1966 did not enter	**1998** did not qualify

The Coach

Bora Milutinovic *Career:* Played for FC Bor (Yugoslavia). Coach of UNAM (Mexico), Udinese (Italy), San Lorenzo (Argentina), UAG (Mexico), Veracruz (Mexico), Mexico, Costa Rica, USA national teams, New York/New Jersey MetroStars (USA), Nigeria national team.
Born: 7 September 1944 *Appointed:* January 2000

Star Performers

Qi Hong *Position:* Forward
Club: Shanghai Shenhua *Born:* 3 June 1976
Zhang Enhua *Position:* Defender
Club: Dalian Shide *Born:* 28 April 1973
An Qi *Position:* Goalkeeper
Club: Dalian Shide *Born:* 21 June 1981
Li Xiaopeng *Position:* Midfield
Club: Shandong Luneng *Born:* 20 June 1975
Fan Zhiyi *Position:* Defender
Club: Dundee (Scotland) *Born:* 22 January 1970

The Road to the Finals

China 10–1 Maldives	Oman 0–2 China
Maldives 0–1 China	Qatar 1–1 China
Cambodia 0–4 China	China 2–0 Uzbekistan
China 5–1 Indonesia	UAE 0–1 China
China 3–1 Cambodia	China 1–0 Oman
Indonesia 0–2 China	China 3–0 Qatar
China 3–0 UAE	Uzbekistan 1–0 China

Here come China – Su Maozhan celebrates his goal in their 3–0 qualifying defeat of Qatar.

Group C

COSTA RICA
Capacity to surprise

World Cup Record

1930	did not enter	**1970**	did not qualify
1934	did not enter	**1974**	did not qualify
1938	withdrew	**1978**	did not qualify
1950	did not enter	**1982**	did not qualify
1954	entry not accepted	**1986**	did not qualify
1958	did not qualify	**1990**	finals 2nd round
1962	did not qualify	**1994**	did not qualify
1966	did not qualify	**1998**	did not qualify

The Coach

Alexander Guimares *Career:* Played for: Deportivo Saprissa. Coached: Belen, Herediano, Deportivo Saprissa, Comunicaciones (Guatemala)
Born: 7 November 1959 *Appointed:* January 2001

Star Performers

Paolo Wanchope *Position:* Striker
Club: Manchester City (England) *Born:* 31 July 1976
Hernan Medford *Position:* Midfield
Club: Necaxa (Mexico) *Born:* 23 May 1968
Rolando Fonseca *Position:* Striker
Club: La Piedad (Mexico) *Born:* 6 June 1974
Gilberto Martinez *Position:* Defender
Club: Deportivo Saprissa *Born:* 1 October 1979
Erick Lonis *Position:* Goalkeeper
Club: Deportivo Saprissa *Born:* 9 September 1965

The Road to the Finals

Barbados 2–1 Costa Rica
Costa Rica 2–1 United States
Costa Rica 2–1 Guatemala
Costa Rica 3–0 Barbados
United States 0–0 Costa Rica
Guatemala 2–1 Costa Rica
Costa Rica 5–2 Guatemala
Costa Rica 2–2 Honduras
Costa Rica 3–0 Trinidad and Tobago
United States 1–0 Costa Rica
Mexico 1–2 Costa Rica
Costa Rica 2–1 Jamaica
Honduras 2–3 Costa Rica
Trinidad and Tobago 0–2 Costa Rica
Costa Rica 2–0 United States
Costa Rica 0–0 Mexico
Jamaica 0–1 Costa Rica

Paolo Wanchope was under great pressure to lead Costa Rica back to the World Cup finals.

In 1990 Costa Rica became the fourth nation from Central America to reach the World Cup finals. In Italy, under legendary coach Bora Milutinovic, Costa Rica made headlines as they exceeded the feats of both Honduras and El Salvador, defeating Scotland 1–0 and Sweden 2–1 in the first round, before losing 4–1 to Czechoslovakia in the second round.

They failed to qualify for the finals in 1994 and 1998, but the 2002 qualifiers provided new hope, built around the talents of 1990 veteran Hernan Medford, midfielder Mauricio Solis, free-kick specialist Ronald Gomez, playmaker Walter Centeno and unpredictable strikers Paulo Wanchope and Rolando Fonseca.

Costa Rica looked out of the running after a 1–0 defeat by Barbados pushed them to the foot of the semi-final qualifying group in the Central and North American region – behind Barbados, the United States and Guatemala.

Pressure on both the squad and Brazilian coach Gilson Nunes rose to almost unbearable proportions. Wanchope had to hire bodyguards to protect his family after threats to their safety while other angry fans threw missiles at the players during training. The worried federation even offered fans a money-back guarantee if Costa Rica did not win their crucial next match against the US.

Not only did they win, by 2–1, but they recovered to reach the final qualifying round – albeit only after beating Guatemala 5–2 in a play-off. The play-off was staged in the Orange Bowl in Miami. Costa Rica went a goal down in three minutes, equalised in the sixth through Wanchope then ran away with further strikes from Fonseca (two), Reinaldo Parks and Jafeth Soto.

New coach works wonders

That took Costa Rica into the final qualifying round from which three nations would go on to Korea and Japan. Mexico and the US were group favourites with Costa Rica rated no more likely to progress than either Honduras, 1998 finalists Jamaica or Trinidad and Tobago, but they did have a new coach in former Deportivo Saprissa boss Alexander Guimares.

Once more, the decisive game was home to the US in front of 24,000 in the Saprissa Stadium in San Jose. Heavy rain before the match upset the Americans but proved no problem for the nimble Fonseca. He had a header cleared off the goal line in the 26th minute then made no mistake from the penalty spot after a trip on Gomez. Fonseca scored his second goal in the 70th minute after beating the American offside trap.

Suddenly the mood in San Jose had changed. No more threats or missiles. Instead the team were feted on a victory parade through the centre of the capital and the government awarded players and coaches a bonus of $200,000.

After enjoying success in 1990, Costa Rica intend to prove the lightning can strike twice.

Group D

SOUTH KOREA
Asia's best bet for glory

World Cup co-hosts South Korea believe they are Asia's strongest football nation. They have the continent's best World Cup record – having qualified in 1954 and the four most recent tournaments. Asian champions in 1954 and 1960, they placed third at the Asian Cup in Lebanon in 2000.

In 1993 South Korea decided to challenge long-time front-runners Japan for the honour of becoming the first Asian hosts for the World Cup. Positive memories of Seoul's staging of the 1988 Olympics plus shrewd political manoeuvring duly earned the

THE COACH

GUUS HIDDINK

Hiddink is appearing at the World Cup finals for a second successive time after taking Holland to the semi-finals in France four years ago. His success earned a lucrative contract with Real Madrid – one of three coaching spells in Spain along with those at Valencia and Betis. Also guided Holland to the quarter-finals of Euro 96.

Koreans joint hosting rights with the Japanese.

Cha Bum Kun is South Korea's best-known player, having enjoyed a lengthy career in the West German Bundesliga. In 1988 he helped Bayer Leverkusen win the UEFA Cup, scoring the crucial aggregate-levelling goal in the second leg of the final against Spain's Español. Cha coached the national team at the 1998 World Cup finals.

In the heart of Seoul is an enormous clock which counts down the days to the Opening Match of the finals in the city's new World Cup Stadium. That clock is a source of pride to the nation, but also a source of pressure for Dutchman Guus Hiddink, South Korea's national coach.

Going Dutch

Hiddink has worked for big clubs in Europe, including Real Madrid and Valencia, and coached Holland to the semi-finals of the 1998 World Cup. Adjusting to Korean culture and lifestyle was not easy for Hiddink or his coaching staff, although it includes Pim Verbeek, who coached in the J.League's second division for several years. At least the Dutchmen have been fortunate in that almost

all their players are on hand, comparatively locally, with clubs in Korea and Japan.

Hiddink noted that Korean players learn quickly. In last year's co-hosted Confederations Cup they improved rapidly game by game – from the 5–0 beating by France to a 2–1 defeat of Mexico and then a 1–0 win against Australia.

The man who matters in defence is Hong Myung-bo. He is the Koreans' captain and sweeper and has been playing in World Cup finals tournaments for a decade. Ahead of him Hiddink will look for inspiration to playmakers Ko Jung-su and Seo Jung-wan as well as forwards Kim Do-hoon, a former top scorer in the Korean league, and Lee Dong-gook, South Korean football's new golden boy.

Lee is one of the few Korean players to have tried their luck in Europe on the strength of his six-goal top-scoring performance at the 2000 Asian Cup in Lebanon. He then played seven matches on loan in Germany with Werder Bremen before returning home to Pohang Steelers in the K-League.

Having helped Pohang win the 1998 Asian Club Championship, Lee knows what international success is all about. The local success of the 2002 World Cup rests on his ability to recreate that winning sensation.

World Cup Record

1930	did not enter	**1970**	did not qualify
1934	did not enter	**1974**	did not qualify
1938	did not enter	**1978**	did not qualify
1950	did not enter	**1982**	did not qualify
1954	finals 1st round	**1986**	finals 1st round
1958	entry not accepted	**1990**	finals 1st round
1962	did not qualify	**1994**	finals 1st round
1966	withdrew	**1998**	finals 1st round

The Coach

Guus Hiddink *Career:* Played for De Graafschap, NEC Nijmegen (both Holland). Coach of PSV Eindhoven (Holland), Real Madrid, Betis, Valencia (all Spain), Holland. *Born:* 8 November 1946 *Appointed:* January 2001

Star Performers

Hong Myung Bo *Position:* Defender
Club: Kashiwa Reysol (Japan) *Born:* 12 February 1969
Seol Ki-Hyun *Position:* Striker
Club: Anderlecht (Belgium) *Born:* 8 January 1979
Ha Seok-ju *Position:* Midfield
Club: Pohang Steelers *Born:* 29 April 1979
Woon Jae Lee *Position:* Goalkeeper
Club: Sangmoo *Born:* 26 April 1973
Sang Chul Yoo *Position:* Defender
Club: Kashiwa Reysol (Japan) *Born:* 18 October 1971

The Road to the Finals

Qualified automatically as hosts

Sang Chul Yoo's commitment typifies South Korea's approach to the 2002 finals – on and off the pitch.

LEE DONG-GOOK

Position: Forward *Club:* Pohang Steelers
Previous clubs: Pohang, Werder Bremen (Ger)
Born: 29 April 1979 *Intl apps:* 43 *Intl goals:* 17

Lee Dong-gook will shoulder the hopes of all South Koreans as he leads the co-hosts' assault on the first round obstacles of Poland, Portugal and the United States. He has the pedigree after finishing top scorer in the 2000 Asian Cup when his six goals in six games lifted Korea to third place. Lee joined top club Pohang Steelers at 17 in 1996 and secured international acclaim two years later when he helped Pohang win the Asian Club Championship and scored the goal which brought South Korea victory in the Asian Youth Cup – by 2–1 over Japan. His exploits earned a six-month trial with German club Werder Bremen in 2001.

Lee Dong-Gook has the breadth of international experience upon which Korea will need to lean heavily.

Group D

World Cup Record

1930	did not enter	**1970**	failed to qualify
1934	failed to qualify	**1974**	failed to qualify
1938	failed to qualify	**1978**	failed to qualify
1950	failed to qualify	**1982**	failed to qualify
1954	failed to qualify	**1986**	finals 1st round
1958	failed to qualify	**1990**	failed to qualify
1962	failed to qualify	**1994**	failed to qualify
1966	third place	**1998**	failed to qualify

The Coach

Antonio Oliveira *Career:* Played for FC Porto, Betis (Spain), Penafiel, Sporting Lisbon, Portugal. Coached Penafiel, Guimaraes, Gil Vicente, Braga, FC Porto, Portugal. *Born:* 10 June 1952 *Appointed:* August 2000

Star Performers

Simao Sabrosa *Position:* Striker
Club: Benfica *Born:* 31 October 1979
Fernando Couto *Position:* Defender
Club: Lazio (Italy) *Born:* 2 August 1969
Nuno Gomes *Position:* Striker
Club: Fiorentina *Born:* 5 July 1976
Rui Costa *Position:* Midfielder
Club: Milan *Born:* 29 March 1972
Sergio Conceiçao *Position:* Midfielder
Club: Juventus *Born:* 15 November 1974

The Road to the Finals

Estonia 1–3 Portugal
Portugal 1–1 Republic of Ireland
Netherlands 0–2 Portugal
Portugal 3–0 Andorra
Portugal 2–2 Netherlands
Republic of Ireland 1–1 Portugal
Portugal 6–0 Cyprus
Andorra 1–7 Portugal
Cyprus 1–3 Portugal
Portugal 5–0 Estonia

Portugal's Frechaut (right) holds the Republic of Ireland's Kevin Kilbane at bay in their 1–1 qualifying draw in Dublin.

PORTUGAL

The romantics' choice

The footballers of Portugal and Brazil both speak the same language on and off the pitch – which is the reason Portugal's return to the World Cup finals is long overdue. Their players boast the most imaginatively delicate technique to be found anywhere in Europe.

The most outstanding exponents such as inspirational forward Luis Figo and playmaker Manuel Rui Costa have long deserved to step out on the greatest stage in the world game. The heroes of Real Madrid and Milan proved the point by leading Portugal to the Euro 2000 semi-finals, rekindling memories of the great days of Eusebio.

The prolific striker from Mozambique was nine-goal top scorer in 1966 when Portugal reached the World Cup finals for the first time and finished third. That team was built around players from Benfica and cross-city

LOOK OUT FOR

LUIS FIGO

Position: Right wing, midfield *Club:* Real Madrid (Sp)
Previous clubs: Sporting, Barcelona (Sp)
Born: 4 November 1972 *Intl apps:* 81 *Intl goals:* 27

Luis Figo, like many of his team-mates from Portugal's world youth cup-winning squad of a decade ago, is approaching his first and last chance of World Cup glory. He does so as one of the most admired Portuguese players since Eusebio. He won league titles with three different clubs in two different countries, was voted European Footballer of the Year after leading Portugal to the semi-finals of Euro 2000 and cost Real Madrid a then world record fee of £35 million when he signed from old rivals Barcelona two years ago. Has been most effective as a traditional right winger at club level, but fills the playmaker's role for his country.

rivals Sporting Lisbon. Today Portugal's best players will be found at some of the finest clubs across the continent.

Portugal lost a penalty shootout in the 1984 European Championship semi-final and in Mexico two years later, they were first-round failures at the World Cup finals. But amends were made shortly afterwards. Under coach Carlos Queiros, Portugal were world youth champions in 1989 and 1991 thanks to teenage talents such as Figo and Rui Costa.

Triumph in adversity

With these two now grown-up internationals, Portugal came off Euro 2000 confident in their own precocious talent but concerned that European group two of the World Cup qualifying tournament matched them against awkward opposition in Holland and the Republic of Ireland. The Portuguese were also weakened by various suspensions after tempers had boiled over in the Euro semi-final defeat by France on a golden goal penalty. Rui Costa, Figo and Ricardo Sa Pinto provided the goals which earned a winning 3–1 start away to Estonia.

A 1–1 home draw against the Irish was disappointing but the subsequent 2–0 defeat of Holland in Rotterdam proved crucial for Portuguese confidence. Even more important was the return match against Holland in Porto. With just seven minutes remaining in normal time, Holland led 2–0, but Pauleta and Figo scored to force a draw.

Controversy was never far away. In the spring of 2001, defensive anchor Fernando Couto – a squad member of the youth team in 1989 – was suspended after failing a dope test in Italy where he played his club football with Lazio. The ban was imposed just before the tough trip to Dublin to face the Irish but his team-mates responded by forcing a 1–1 draw, courtesy of an equaliser from Figo.

This was the vital result because the Federação Portuguesa de Futebol had judged the group fixture negotiations perfectly. Their closing four matches were all against group minnows in Cyprus (twice), Andorra and Estonia. Portugal won all four matches, scoring 21 goals and conceding two. They finished level on points with the Republic of Ireland but predictably topped the group – and qualified direct for the finals – on goal difference.

Luis Figo is perfectly balanced as he strikes Portugal's superb first goal – past the attempted block of Tony Adams – in their 3–2 comeback victory over England at Eindhoven in Euro 2000.

Group D

POLAND

Back in the big time

Between 1974 and 1986, Poland were one of the most successful nations in the World Cup, finishing third twice, and reaching the second round twice more. In 2002, just as in 1974, the Poles may be unconsidered, but they have the talent to surprise.

Poland will be back at the World Cup finals for the first time since they crashed out to Brazil in the second round in Mexico in 1986. Polish football went into freefall in the wake of that defeat. Problems caused by a dearth of youthful talent were exacerbated by the financial crisis provoked by the break-up of the last controlling fragments of the Communist system.

World Cups and European Championships went ahead without any contribution from the nation which had impressed the game with talents such as Kaziu Deyna, Grzegorz Lato, Wlodek Lubanski and the flame-haired Zbigniew Boniek.

Remarkably, however, the revival has been led by a Nigerian. Emmanuel Olisadebe never made the national squad back home but he proved a sensation after gambling his ambitions on a transfer to Poland's Polonia Warsaw. His goals led Polonia to the league title and earned Olisadebe a fast-track route to first a Polish passport and then a place in the national team's attack.

Sensational start

His World Cup debut was equally sensational. Poland began their European group five campaign in September 2000 in the testing atmosphere of the Republic Stadium in Kiev, Ukraine. The nerveless Olisadebe scored twice – his first after only three minutes – in the 3–1 win over Ukraine. The succeeding nine months brought Poland and their new hero four more victories and two draws, top place in the group and a five-point advantage over Belarus. Olisadebe proved unstoppable by snatching another two goals in an away win over the disappointing Norway.

He also struck in the 3–0 home win over the Norwegians which ensured Poland would top the group with two rounds of

matches to go. Safe in the knowledge that they had already qualified, Poland were complacent against Belarus, which prompted a 4–1 defeat – the Poles' only group defeat – and a mere 1–1 home draw against Ukraine. Coach Jerzy Engel was not amused, but Poland's fans and media ignored any possible warning signs in their delight at returning, after 16 years, to the World Cup finals.

The present team may not boast players with the reputation of the likes of Deyna, Lato, Lubanski or Boniek, but goalkeeeer Jerzy Dudek is considered one of the best in Europe, and he has quickly become a fan favourite at Liverpool. The Polish League is not one of Europe's strongest, as evidenced by the fact Olisadebe now plays for Panathinaikos of Greece, playmaker Piotr Swierczewski is in France with Bastia, defender Tomasz Waldoch plays for Schalke '04 in Germany's Bundesliga

Boniek will be back on national team duty in Korea and Japan. Not as a player but wielding influence, even so, as vice-president of the Polish federation.

World Cup Record

1930	did not enter	**1970**	did not qualify
1934	withdrew	**1974**	third place
1938	first round	**1978**	finals 2nd round
1950	did not enter	**1982**	third place
1954	withdrew	**1986**	finals 2nd round
1958	did not qualify	**1990**	did not qualify
1962	did not qualify	**1994**	did not qualify
1966	did not qualify	**1998**	did not qualify

The Coach

Jerzy Engel *Career:* Played for Polonia Warsaw, Coach of Polonia Warsaw, Legia Warsaw, Apollon Limassol (Cyprus), Apop Paphos (Cyprus), Nea Salami (Cyprus), Legia, Aris Limassol (Cyprus), Nea, Polonia
Born: 6 October 1952 *Appointed:* January 2000

Star Performers

Jerzy Dudek *Position:* goalkeeper
Club: Liverpool (England) *Born:* 23 March 1973
Emmanuel Olisadebe *Position:* Striker
Club: Panathinaikos (Greece) *Born:* 22 December 1978
Tomasz Waldoch *Position:* Defender
Club: Schalke '04 (Germany) *Born:* 10 May 1970
Michael Zewlakow *Position:* Defender
Club: Excelsior Mouscron (Belgium) *Born:* 22 April 1976
Piotr Swierczewski *Position:* Midfielder
Club: Marseille (France) *Born:* 8 April1978

The Road to the Finals

Ukraine 1–3 Poland	Wales 1–2 Poland
Poland 3–1 Belarus	Armenia 1–1 Poland
Poland 0–0 Wales	Poland 3–0 Norway
Norway 2–3 Poland	Belarus 4–1 Poland
Poland 4–0 Armenia	Poland 1–1 Ukraine

Poland's Nigerian-born striker Emmanuel Olasidebe forces his way past Wales's Kit Symons.

UNITED STATES
Looking for respect

Group D

World Cup Record

1930	semi-final	**1970**	did not qualify
1934	finals 1st round	**1974**	did not qualify
1938	withdrew	**1978**	did not qualify
1950	finals 1st round	**1982**	did not qualify
1954	did not qualify	**1986**	did not qualify
1958	did not qualify	**1990**	finals 1st round
1962	did not qualify	**1994**	finals 2nd round
1966	did not qualify	**1998**	finals 1st round

The Coach

Bruce Arena *Career:* Played for Nassau City College, Tacoma Tides, US national team. Coached University of Puget Sound, University of Virginia, US Olympic squad, Washington DC United.
Born: 21 September 1951 *Appointed:* October 1998

Star Performers

Claudio Reyna *Position:* Midfield
Club: Sunderland (England) *Born:* 20 July 1973
Joe-Max Moore *Position:* Striker
Club: Everton (England) *Born:* 23 February 1971
Earnie Stewart *Position:* Striker
Club: NAC Breda (Holland) *Born:* 28 September 1969
Jeff Agoos *Position:* Defender
Club: San Jose Earthquakes *Born:* 5 February 1968
David Regis *Position:* Defender
Club: Metz (France) *Born:* 2 December 1968

The Road to the Finals

Guatemala 1–1 USA	USA 1–0 Costa Rica
Costa Rica 2–1 USA	Jamaica 0–0 USA
USA 7–0 Barbados	USA 2–0 Trinidad & Tob
USA 1–0 Guatemala	Mexico 1–0 USA
USA 0–0 Costa Rica	USA 2–3 Honduras
Barbados 0–4 USA	Costa Rica 2–0 USA
USA 2–0 Mexico	USA 2–1 Jamaica
Honduras 1–2 USA	Trinidad & Tob 0–0 USA

Cobi Jones gives the USA wings in their decisive 2–1 victory over Jamaica in Foxboro.

The United States were long considered a joke in international soccer circles. But they reached the inaugural World Cup semi-finals in 1930 and England were not laughing when they fell 1–0 to the USA in 1950. Indeed the 2002 finals will the fourth in a row for the USA, a run current holders France have never enjoyed.

Opponents who underestimate the Americans will be making a serious mistake. The USA have an ever-deeper well of young football talent from which to draw. They proved the point when a team including high-potential Landon Donovan and DaMarcus Beasley finished fourth at the World Under-17 Championship in New Zealand in 2000.

At senior level coach Steve Sampson had been replaced immediately after the USA had been eliminated in the first round in the 1998 finals. Bruce Arena, the most successful club coach in the American game, took over. His four-year tenure means he is one of the longest-serving managers at the 2002 finals. Arena's faith in home-grown talent has been demonstrated by his selection of around 90 players for his national squad training camps in his first three years in charge.

Home comforts

In the CONCACAF region, the USA were seeded direct into semi-final qualifying group E. They lost only one of their six games and finished a point clear at the top of the table with 14 goals scored and only three conceded. But 11 of those goals were scored home and away against Barbados with Earnie Stewart the three-goal top scorer and two each coming from Ante Razov, Brian McBride and Joe-Max Moore.

The final round did not go as planned. With two games to play, it appeared the USA needed to beat both Jamaica and Trinidad and Tobago to secure a place in Korea and Japan. Fortunately Honduras lost 1–0 at home to Trinidad and Mexico drew with Costa Rica so, simultaneously, a 2–1 win over Jamaica saw the USA safely through to the finals. Moore, who plays in England for Everton, scored both goals, the first after just four minutes and the other a penalty with nine minutes remaining.

Apart from the 1950 victory over England, USA soccer was long famed for the controversial North American Soccer League which attracted top foreign veterans such as Pele, Franz Beckenbauer, Johan Cruyff and George Best. The NASL collapsed in the late 1980s to be succeeded – after nearly a decade without a professional eleven-a-side league – by the more durable Major League Soccer which had been founded on the back of the success of the American-hosted 1994 World Cup.

The USA women's team have twice won their World Cup. The men dream of emulating them. But 2002 is probably a little too soon.

Group E

GERMANY
In rebuilding mode

World Cup Record

1930	did not enter	**1970**	third place
1934	third place	**1974**	champions
1938	finals 1st round	**1978**	finals 2nd round
1950	did not enter	**1982**	runners-up
1954	champions	**1986**	runners-up
1958	fourth place	**1990**	champions
1962	quarter-finals	**1994**	quarter-finals
1966	runners-up	**1998**	quarter-finals

The Coach

Rudi Völler *Career:* Played for Kickers Offenbach, 1860 Munich, Werder Bremen, Roma (Italy), Marseille (France), Bayer Leverkusen. Coach of Bayer Leverkusen. *Born:* 13 April 1960 *Appointed:* July 2000

Star Performers

Jens Novotny *Position:* Sweeper
Club: Bayer Leverkusen *Born:* 11 January 1974
Dietmar Hamann *Position:* Midfielder
Club: Liverpool (England) *Born:* 27 August 1973
Michael Ballack *Position:* Midfielder
Club: Bayer Leverkusen *Born:* 26 September 1976
Sebastian Deisler *Position:* Defender
Club: Herta Berlin *Born:* 5 January 1980
Carsten Jancker *Position:* Forward
Club: Bayern Munich *Born:* 28 August 1974

The Road to the Finals

Germany 2–0 Greece	Albania 0–2 Germany
England 0–1 Germany	Germany 1–5 England
Germany 2–1 Albania	Germany 0–0 Finland
Greece 2–4 Germany	Ukraine 1–1 Germany
Finland 2–2 Germany	Germany 4–1 Ukraine

Oliver Neuville celebrates after scoring Germany's second goal in their 4–1 play-off victory against Ukraine in Dortmund.

Coach Rudi Völler, a World Cup-winning centre-forward in 1990, faces a huge task in Japan and South Korea. Great national pride demands that he comes up with a team and tactics to prove worthy of German football's illustrious past and its exciting future.

Germany's progress to the finals was nothing like as smooth as appeared likely after they opened their qualifying campaign with a 1–0 win over England at Wembley. Liverpool midfielder Dietmar Hamann scored to upset England's plans for a winning shutdown of Wembley stadium. Victory prompted the departure of England boss Kevin Keegan.

THE COACH
RUDI VÖLLER

Völler played centre-forward when Germany won the World Cup in 1990 and enjoyed an outstanding club career with Werder Bremen and Roma. Later became general manager of Bayer Leverkusen who loaned him to the federation to be caretaker manager in 2000–01. Stayed on after a doping scandal ruled out his nominated successor, Christoph Daum.

But victory masked problems within the German camp which were laid bare a year later when England hammered out a 5–1 revenge victory in Munich's Olympic stadium. Germany could still have qualified direct for the finals had they won at home to Finland in their last group nine game but a goalless draw left them as runners-up and pushed them into a play-off against Ukraine instead.

The embarrassment was exacerbated by the fact that the German federation, expecting to win the group, had agreed to play South Korea in early November in a friendly to open the Seoul World Cup Stadium. Hastily the Germans made their apologies – the stadium-opening honour fell to Croatia instead – and went off to do battle in Kiev and Dortmund.

Bayer Leverkusen's Michael Ballack, one of the Munich culprits, turned national hero overnight. He scored the goal which earned Germany a 1–1 draw in the Ukraine and then struck twice in the 4–1 victory in the second leg. Germany, after all, had maintained their proud record of never having failed the World Cup qualifying test.

Whether the present generation of stars – Ballack, Sebastian Deisler, Oliver Kahn and company – can match the achievements of their predecessors is another matter.

Germany, triple world champions boast a remarkable record.

An enviable record

They were third in 1934, their World Cup debut, and winners for the first time in 1954. The arrival of Franz Beckenbauer signalled an amazing run: runners-up in 1966, third in 1970, and winners in 1975. As coach he took them to victory again 1990, this after Germany had lost in the Final in 1982 and 1986. Germany have enjoyed similar success in the European Championship with three wins and two defeats in the Final. At club level, Bayern Munich, Borussia Dortmund and Hamburg have all been European Champions.

The historical circle was finally closed in the early 1990s with the return to the national fold of the former East Germany – complete with outstanding players such as Matthias Sammer, Ulf Kirsten, Thomas Doll and Andreas Thom.

Even off the pitch the success story has been maintained with Franz Beckenbauer now a vice-president of the German federation, leading the campaign which secured host rights to the World Cup in 2006.

OLIVER KAHN

Position: Goalkeeper   *Club:* Bayern Munich
Previous club: Karlsruhe
Born: 15 June 1969   *Intl apps:* 41   *Intl goals:* –

Oliver Kahn is the latest in a long, proud line of defiant German goalkeepers and a worthy pupil and successor to Bayern Munich's 1974 World Cup winner, Sepp Maier. Kahn made his name with Karlsruhe and went first to the World Cup in 1994 but was not given a game in the United States. Transferring to Bayern changed everything. He overtook Andreas Kopke and Jens Lehmann to become Germany's No. 1 and was twice voted Footballer of the Year. The second award followed an outstanding 2000–01 season when he played a decisive role as Bayern beat Valencia on penalties to win the Champions League Final.

Oliver Kahn gets the better of England's Nick Barmby for once in Germany's shock 5–1 defeat in Munich last September.

Cup finalists, in front of 120,000 fans in Tehran and without inspirational, injured Roy Keane was a major challenge. The Irish also carried with them the painful knowledge that they had missed out on the last three major tournaments because of play-off defeats to Holland, Belgium and Turkey.

But they took a solid record of achievement to Tehran – unbeaten in 16 matches, unbeaten in 11 away games, and defeated only five times in 33 competitive matches since McCarthy succeeded Jack Charlton as manager. Defeat No. 6 was, however, only by 1–0 and McCarthy's men thus qualified for the World Cup finals for the first time since 1994.

Newcastle goalkeeper Shay Given proved the sharpness of his reflexes with several magnificent saves in Tehran; record inter-

IRELAND
Ireland going for more than Craic

The magnitude of the Republic of Ireland's achievement in reaching Korea and Japan is best demonstrated by the fact that Roy Keane, Niall Quinn and Steve Staunton earned the team's ticket while the likes of Holland's much-vaunted Patrick Kluivert, Edgar Davids and the De Boer twins did not.

Not that Republic of Ireland manager Mick McCarthy felt any sense of guilt at having derailed one of the most popular of international nations. He knew that his men had earned their dream reward.

The Irish began the group as outsiders with Portugal and Holland favourites to fill the top two places. But the Dutch should have been warned when, in the very first mainstream matchday, they had to come back from 2–0 to the Irish to force a 2–2 draw in Amsterdam.

Next time out Ireland forced a 1–1 draw away to Portugal and the bandwagon was well under way. When McAteer struck another key goal to defeat Holland in Dublin in September 2001 the writing was on the wall for the Dutch. Portugal topped the group with Ireland in second place and bound, by the luck of the draw, to face Asian hopefuls Iran in the intercontinental qualifying play-offs.

Fourth time lucky

Goals from Robbie Keane and Ian Harte produced a 2–0 victory at Lansdowne Road in the first leg. But facing Iran, 1998 World

World Cup Record

1930	did not enter	**1970**	did not qualify
1934	did not qualify	**1974**	did not qualify
1938	did not qualify	**1978**	did not qualify
1950	did not qualify	**1982**	did not qualify
1954	did not qualify	**1986**	did not qualify
1958	did not qualify	**1990**	quarter-finals
1962	did not qualify	**1994**	finals 2nd round
1966	did not qualify	**1998**	did not qualify

The Coach

Mick McCarthy _Career:_ Played for Barnsley (England), Manchester City (England), Celtic (Scotland), Lyon (France), Millwall (England), Republic of Ireland national team. Coach of Millwall (England).
Born: 7 February 1959 _Appointed:_ March 1996

Star Performers

Steve Staunton _Position:_ Defender
Club: Aston Villa (England) _Born:_ 19 January 1969
Robbie Keane _Position:_ Striker
Club: Leeds United (England) _Born:_ 8 August 1980
Shay Given _Position:_ Goalkeeper
Club: Newcastle United (England) _Born:_ 20 April 1976
Ian Harte _Position:_ Defender
Club: Leeds United (England) _Born:_ 31 August 1977
Damien Duff _Position:_ Midfielder
Club: Blackburn Rovers (Greece) _Born:_ 2 March 1979

The Road to the Finals

Holland 2–2 Republic of Ireland
Portugal 1–1 Republic of Ireland
Republic of Ireland 2–0 Estonia
Cyprus 0–4 Republic of Ireland
Andorra 0–3 Republic of Ireland
Republic of Ireland 3–1 Andorra
Republic of Ireland 1–1 Portugal
Estonia 0–2 Republic of Ireland
Republic of Ireland 1–0 Holland
Republic of Ireland 4–0 Cyprus
Republic of Ireland 2–0 Iran
Iran 1–0 Republic of Ireland

**Ian Harte (3) scores the first of the Republic of Ireland's two goals in their play-off duel with Iran in Dublin.**

ROY KEANE

Position: Midfield *Club:* Manchester Utd (England)
Previous clubs: Cobh Ramblers, Nottingham Forest (England)
Born: 10 August 1971 *Intl apps:* 56 *Intl goals:* 9

Roy Keane is the finest midfield anchor in British football today. He was perhaps Brian Clough's greatest bargain after costing Nottingham Forest only £10,000 from Cobh Ramblers in 1989–90, long after Forest had enjoyed their European glory. Keane made amends after joining Manchester United for £3.75 million in 1993. The fierce competitive spirit which has driven team-mates to success has brought personal cost: club captain Keane missed United's dramatic Champions League Final win over Bayern Munich in 1999 through suspension. He has proved equally uncompromising verbally and physically – as proved by trenchant criticisms of fans and team-mates down the years.

Roy Keane battled through an injury to drive the Republic of Ireland to their invaluable home victory over Iran at Lansdowne Road last November.

national Steve Staunton provides experience at the centre of defence while Leeds' fullback Harte offers an extra surprise weapon with his powerful free kicks. In midfield Roy Keane is acknowledged as one of European football's most effective anchor-men and namesake Robbie Keane, up front, is among the most talented of the new generation.

Remarkably, it was only in 1990, in Italy, that the Republic of Ireland made their World Cup finals debut and reached the quarter-finals before falling to their hosts. McCarthy played centre back in all five matches. Four years later they defeated Italy in the group stage, but Holland knocked them out in the second round.

Once again, opponents in Japan and Korea will underestimate McCarthy and his team at their peril.

MICK MCCARTHY

McCarthy was a rock in the Irish Republic's defence under Jack Charlton whom he ultimately succeeded after a four-year spell as manager of Millwall. Missed out on the 1998 World Cup and Euro 2000 after play-off defeats but it was third time lucky against Iran last November. McCarthy's playing career included a Scottish League title with Celtic.

CAMEROON
The cream of African football

Group E

World Cup Record

1930	did not enter	**1970**	did not qualify
1934	did not enter	**1974**	did not qualify
1938	did not enter	**1978**	did not qualify
1950	did not enter	**1982**	finals 1st round
1954	did not enter	**1986**	did not qualify
1958	did not enter	**1990**	quarter-finals
1962	did not enter	**1994**	finals 1st round
1966	withdrew	**1998**	finals 1st round

The Coach

Winfried Schäfer *Career:* Played for Kickers Offenbach, Borussia Mönchengladbach, Karlsruhe (all West Germany). Coach of Borussia Mönchengladbach, Karlsruhe, Stuttgart, Tennis Borussia Berlin (all West Germany).
Born: 10 January 1950 *Appointed:* September 2001

Star Performers

Patrick Mboma *Position:* Striker
Club: Parma (Italy) *Born:* 15 November 1970
Samuel Eto'o *Position:* Striker
Club: Real Mallorca (Spain) *Born:* 10 March 1981
Marc-Vivien Foe *Position:* Midfield
Club: Olympique Lyonnais (France) *Born:* 1 May 1975
Rigobert Song *Position:* Defender
Club: West Ham United (England) *Born:* 1 July 1976
Jacques Songo'o *Position:* Goalkeeper
Club: Metz (France) *Born:* 17 March 1964

The Road to the Finals

Somalia 0–3 Cameroon	Cameroon 1–0 Zambia
Cameroon 3–0 Somalia	Cameroon 1–0 Libya
Libya 0–3 Cameroon	Angola 2–0 Cameroon
Cameroon 3–0 Angola	Cameroon 2–0 Togo
Togo 0–2 Cameroon	Zambia 2–2 Cameroon

All-powerful Patrick Mboma leads Cameroon to their 2000 Olympic Games gold-medal triumph over Spain in Sydney.

Cameroon are the most successful African nation in the history of the World Cup finals. Their first qualifying attempt came for the 1970 tournament and 2002 sees the Indomitable Lions' fifth trip to the finals, the fourth in succession.

They first reached the finals in 1982, returning home undefeated after three draws, including holding eventual champions Italy to a 1–1 stalemate. A 1–0 win over Diego Maradona's Argentine world champions in the 1990 Opening Match made headlines. Cameroon went on to reach the quarter-finals, the only nation from outside Europe or South America to reach the last eight since 1970. They lost narrowly to England but goalkeeper Thomas N'Kono and centre-forward Roger Milla earned worldwide fame.

Cameroon qualified for the 1994 World Cup, but the players' naïve readiness to believe their own over-ambitious publicity was all too clear. They crashed out in the first round after losing 3–0 to Brazil and 6–1 to Russia. First-round failure was again their fate at France 98.

Yet two years later the national team scored a spectacular double. Not only did they win the gold medal at the Sydney Olympic Games but also they completed a hat-trick of African Nations Cup victories. Victory over co-hosts Nigeria, on penalties, followed earlier victories in 1984 and 1988.

World travellers

Home, for Cameroon footballers, can be anywhere within the football world. Almost half of the 1994 squad were playing in Europe or Asia as were no fewer than 17 of their 22-man squad in 1998. The exile contingent might be even higher in South Korea and Japan led by 2000 African Footballer of the Year Patrick Mboma – who knows Japan well after a stint in the J.League with Gamba Osaka.

Mboma scored Cameroon's first goal in the 2002 Cup when he struck after 26 minutes of the first leg of their opening round 6–0 aggregate victory over Somalia. He duly added five more goals in the group phase in which the Indomitable Lions were beaten only once, by 2–0 away to Angola.

In the end they secured their place in the finals with a match to play, courtesy of a 2–0 home win over Togo. Samuel Eto'o of Mallorca and Marc-Vivien Foe of Lyon scored the goals which sent the nation wild with pride and delight.

Cameroon's record was impressive. They won eight matches, drew one and lost one, scoring 20 goals and conceding four, despite managerial chaos. Pierre Lechantre was replaced by Jean-Paul Akono, then recalled only to be replaced again, by fellow Frenchman Robert Corfou, only for the German Winfried Schäfer to take over after qualification in September 2001.

Rigobert Song and Raymond Kalla in defence, Foe and Geremi in midfield, Mboma and Eto'o in attack, guarantee that Cameroon will be one of the best-balanced teams competing in the 2002 finals.

Group E

Coaching merry-go-round

Not that they had a smooth ride through the final qualifying round. The Saudis drew their opening fixture against Bahrain then went down 2–0 to Iran in Tehran. Santrac was dismissed and Al Johar was reinstated. The gamble paid off. Saudi Arabia beat Iraq in Bahrain and followed up with two more victories before drawing with Iran in Jeddah.

Two goals from Abdullah bin Shehan earned victory over Iraq in Amman, Jordan. Then further strikes from bin Shehan, Abdullah Jumaan, Al Jaber and Ibrahim Mater added up to the crucial 4–1 win over Thailand – coupled with Iran's shock defeat by Bahrain – secured the Saudis' ticket to the finals.

Al Temyat intends to be back on duty for the finals in Korea and Japan. As he said: "Despite the fact that most of our team are still quite young, we have some highly talented players. We consider ourselves as responsible for building on the successes of the squads who reached the last two World Cups."

SAUDI ARABIA
Building on recent success

Saudi Arabian football burst onto the world map in 1994. At the World Cup finals in the USA, Saeed Owairan contributed one of the finest solo goals in World Cup history, dribbling from inside his own half to score in a 1–0 win against Belgium.

That marked Saudi Arabia's World Cup finals debut and they reached the second round. Four years later, however, they crashed out in the first round. Now Korea and Japan marks finals appearance No. 3 and a chance to prove they belong.

Saudi Arabia are one of the emergent nations of Asian football and with untold oil-based wealth at their disposal, could come to dominate the region's football as the Koreans and the Iranians have. The Saudis' first honours came in the 1980s, when they won the 1984 and 1988 Asian Championships. Simultaneously they invested heavily in developing the domestic football infrastructure and building the magnificent King Fahd stadium in Riyadh which ranks among the finest in the world.

Their confidence, in the qualifying campaign for 2002, was undermined by a knee injury which sidelined Asian Player of the Year Nawaf Al Temyat. But coach Nasser Al Johar had few problems guiding his men past Vietnam, Bangladesh and Mongola in the first qualifying round before handing over the reins to Yugoslav coach Slobodan Santrac.

Saudi Arabia were revealed as far more than a one-man team. Mohammed Al Daeyea has long been considered the finest goalkeeper in the Gulf region while Mohammed Al Khilaiwi has totalled more than 140 international appearances at the heart of central defence. In attack the experience of one-time Wolverhampton Wanderers forward Sami Al Jaber is balanced by the potential and power of Talal Al Meshal who scored three times when the Saudis finished runners-up in the last Asian Cup finals in 2000.

World Cup Record

1930	did not enter	**1970**	did not enter
1934	did not enter	**1974**	did not enter
1938	did not enter	**1978**	did not qualify
1950	did not enter	**1982**	did not qualify
1954	did not enter	**1986**	did not qualify
1958	did not enter	**1990**	did not qualify
1962	did not enter	**1994**	finals 2nd round
1966	did not enter	**1998**	finals 1st round

The Coach

Nasser Al Johar *Career:* Coach of Saudi Arabia youth teams.
Born: 4 March 1961 *Appointed:* July 2001

Star Performers

Sami Al Jaber *Position:* Midfield
Club: Al Hilal *Born:* 11 December 1972
Abdullah al-Shehan *Position:* Striker
Club: Al Shabab *Born:* 29 September 1975
Obaid Al Dosary *Position:* Midfield
Club: Al-Ahly *Born:* 2 October 1975
Mohammed Al Daeyea *Position:* Goalkeeper
Club: Al Hilal *Born:* 2 August 1972
Nawaf Al Temyat *Position:* Midfield
Club: Al Hilal *Born:* 28 June 1976

The Road to the Finals

Saudi Arabia 6–0 Mongolia	Iran 2–0 Saudi Arabia
Bangladesh 0–3 Saudi Arabia	Saudi Arabia 1–0 Iraq
Saudi Arabia 5–0 Vietnam	Thailand 1–3 Saudi Arabia
Mongolia 0–6 Saudi Arabia	Bahrain 0–4 Saudi Arabia
Saudi Arabia 6–0 Bangladesh	Saudi Arabia 2–2 Iran
Vietnam 0–4 Saudi Arabia	Iraq Saudi1–2 Arabia
Saudi Arabia 1–1 Bahrain	Saudi Arabia 4–1 Thailand

Saudi Arabia's Sami Al-Jaber splits the Iranian defence down the middle during their 2–2 draw at the Youth Welfare Stadium, Jeddah in September 2001.

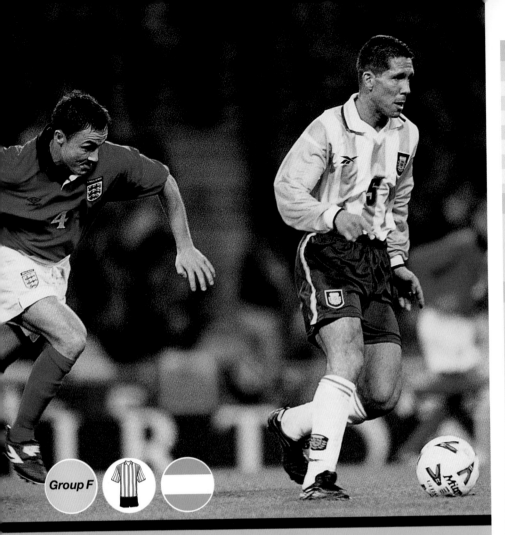

Group F

World Cup Record

1930	runners-up	**1970**	did not qualify
1934	did not enter	**1974**	finals 2nd round
1938	withdrew	**1978**	winners
1950	withdrew	**1982**	finals 2nd round
1954	did not enter	**1986**	winners
1958	finals 1st round	**1990**	runners-up
1962	finals 1st round	**1994**	finals 2nd round
1966	quarter-final	**1998**	quarter-final

The Coach

Marcelo Bielsa *Career:* Played for Newells Old Boys, Cordoba, Rosario. Coached Newells Old Boys, Velez Sarsfield, Atlas, America (both Mexico), Espanyol (Spain). *Born:* 21 July 1955 *Appointed:* September 1998

Star Performers

Walter Samuel *Position:* Central defender
Club: Roma (Italy) *Born:* 23 March 1978
Ariel Ortega *Position:* Striker
Club: River Plate *Born:* 4 March 1974
Juan Sorin *Position:* Defender
Club: Cruzeiro (Brazil) *Born:* 5 May 1976
Hernan Crespo *Position:* Striker
Club: Lazio (Italy) *Born:* 5 July 1975
Gustavo Lopez *Position:* Midfield
Club: Celta Vigo (Spain) *Born:* 13 April 1973

The Road to the Finals

Argentina 4–1 Chile	Chile 0–2 Argentina
Venezuela 0–4 Argentina	Argentina 5–0 Venezuela
Argentina 1–0 Bolivia	Bolivia 3–3 Argentina
Colombia 1–3 Argentina	Argentina 3–0 Colombia
Argentina 2–0 Ecuador	Ecuador 0–2 Argentina
Brazil 3–1 Argentina	Argentina 2–1 Brazil
Argentina 1–1 Paraguay	Paraguay 2–2 Argentina
Peru 1–2 Argentina	Argentina 2–0 Peru
Argentina 2–1 Uruguay	Uruguay 1–1 Argentina

Diego Simeone (right), Argentine scourge of England, leaves Dennis Wise trailing in the countries' last friendly.

ARGENTINA
Favourites for glory

As double World Cup winners, Argentina know what it takes to succeed. With world-class players in many positions, there is a good chance that Argentina will be celebrating in Yokohama on 30 June.

Argentina were winners in 1978, as hosts, and 1986, in Mexico, during which time they provided the game with the most stridently controversial player of the modern era – Diego Maradona. They now lead the South American World Cup challenge, rather than long-time rivals Brazil.

The manner in which they ran away with the arduously long – 18-game – South American qualifying group for 2002 and the weight of attacking talent mean that coach Marcelo Bielsa's men need fear no comparisons with illustrious predecessors.

Bielsa was comparatively unknown at home. He had never coached one of the club giants such as Boca Juniors or River Plate. Instead he was recalled from Espanyol in

Spain, and he has relied heavily on "exiles" based in Europe rather than the current and highly-talented crop of domestic heroes.

Argentina made the perfect start, thrashing Chile 4–1 in Buenos Aires and leaving no doubts that they intended to grab their ticket for Korea and Japan as quickly as possible. Gabriel Batistuta, Juan Veron (two) and Claudio Lopez – all European-based – scored the goals.

Only two of the starting line-up – keeper Roberto Bonano and centre-back Walter Samuel – were not playing in Europe but, within 16 months, they too had signed for European clubs. In fact, European club demands and distractions have always been a problem for Argentina. But they now benefit from FIFA's enforcement of greater uniformity in World Cup qualifying schedules.

They followed up the Chile win with four further victories until two setbacks slowed them – a 3–1 defeat in Brazil in Sao Paulo and a 1–1 home draw against Paraguay.

These proved only minor hitches along the way, however. Argentina regained winning style against Peru, Uruguay, Chile, again, and Venezuela.

Cruise control

The group was far from over but Argentina – with 28 points from 11 games – could cruise the rest of the way. They did so despite

THE COACH
MARCELO BIELSA

Bielsa, a former central defender from Rosario, had coached in three countries before being appointed as successor to Daniel Passarella after the 1998 World Cup exit. He worked in Argentine club football with Newells Old Boys and Velez Sarsfield, in Mexico with Atlas and America and then in Spain with Espanyol, the second club in the city of Barcelona.

Bielsa's decision to overlook record national team marksman Batistuta because of a string of niggling injuries.

With Hernan Crespo happy to step into the breach and Javier Saviola in reserve, Bielsa had no need to worry. Midfield is top-heavy with creative talent, courtesy of Veron, Marcelo Gallardo and Ariel Ortega.

Indeed, so talented is the midfield that there was rarely a place in the starting line-up for Boca Juniors' Juan Roman Riquelme – who was voted South American Footballer of the Year for 2001, ahead of the likes of Ortega and "wonderboy" Andres d'Alessandro. Bielsa's only concerns may thus centre on goalkeeper and defence –

and keeping Argentina's notoriously short-fuse temper under control.

Argentina are justifiably proud of their record at national and club level. As well as their two championships, they were runners-up to Uruguay in the inaugural World Cup in 1930, and were second to West Germany in 1990. They have won the Copa America 14 times while, at club level, Argentina boast no fewer than six different World Club Cup winners.

No wonder they believe history is on their side in Korea and Japan.

Juan Sebastian Veron powers through the Peruvian defence during the 2–0 win with which Argentina wrapped up their qualifying campaign.

Group F

ENGLAND
Relying on young talent

England, in 2000–01, proved beyond all doubt that a year is a long time in football. On 11 October 2000, they had no coach, no goals and one point, to lie bottom of World Cup Qualifying Group 9; on 6 October 2001, five wins and one draw later, they were group winners.

The campaign opened with a 1–0 defeat at the hands of old rivals Germany at Wembley. The last match in the famous old stadium should have been the springboard to a bright new era, after the disappointment of Euro 2000. Instead defeat marked not only a depressing end to the Wembley era but also the end of Kevin Keegan's managerial reign. He resigned within minutes of the final whistle.

The media which had played such an enthusiastic role in Keegan's original

appointment condemned him and the soccer soul-searching clouded the managerial caretaker reigns of Howard Wilkinson and Peter Taylor. Even the revolutionary decision to sign up England's first foreign manager, in

THE COACH
SVEN-GORAN ERIKSSON
Turned to coaching after injury forced his premature retirement as a player. Won the UEFA Cup with IFK Gothenburg and collected a string of league titles and cups in Portugal and Italy with Benfica, Roma, Fiorentina, Sampdoria and Lazio. On succeeding caretaker Peter Taylor, he became the first foreigner to manage England.

Sven-Goran Eriksson, was questioned.

Eriksson quickly made his presence felt. England won their first six matches under his command and David Beckham emerged as an inspirational captain. The need to go "on the road" after Wembley's decommissioning delivered a remarkable new bond between players and fans.

"New England" beat Finland 2–1 at Anfield, Albania 3–1 in Tirana and Greece 2–0 in Athens. They went into summer 2001 six points behind Germany at the top of the group – with a game in hand – but they were bound, at the least, for a play-off opportunity to reach the finals.

New crop brings rich harvest
Eriksson had to undergo a fast-track education course in English football. He

54

World Cup Record

1930	did not enter	1970	quarter-final
1934	did not enter	1974	did not qualify
1938	did not enter	1978	did not qualify
1950	finals 1st round	1982	finals 2nd round
1954	quarter-final	1986	quarter-final
1958	finals 1st round	1990	4th place
1962	quarter-final	1994	failed to qualify
1966	winners	1998	finals 2nd round

The Coach

Sven-Göran Eriksson *Career:* Coach of Degerfors (Sweden), IFK Gothenburg (Sweden), Benfica (Portugal), Roma (Italy), Fiorentina (Italy), Benfica (Portugal), Sampdoria (Italy), Lazio (Italy).
Born: 9 February 1954 *Appointed:* January 2001

Star Performers

Steve McManaman *Position:* Winger
Club: Real Madrid (Spain) *Born:* 11 February 1972
Paul Scholes *Position:* Midfielder
Club: Manchester United *Born:* 16 November 1974
Michael Owen *Position:* Striker
Club: Liverpool *Born:* 14 December 1979
Steven Gerrard *Position:* Midfielder
Club: Liverpool *Born:* 30 May 1980
Sol Campbell *Position:* Defender
Club: Arsenal *Born:* 18 September 1974

The Road to the Finals

England 0–1 Germany	Greece 0–2 England
Finland 0–0 England	Germany 1–5 England
England 2–1 Finland	England 2–0 Albania
Albania 1–3 England	England 2–2 Greece

Opposite: Steven Gerrard scores the second of England's five goals in their sensational 5–1 victory over Germany in Munich.

discovered that England was blessed with, potentially, one of its finest flowerings of young talent for years. Rio Ferdinand and Ashley Cole in defence, Steven Gerrard plus Beckham and Paul Scholes in midfield and the voracious Michael Owen up front made England the envy of the rest of the Europe in general and Germany in particular – especially after 1 September last year.

That was when Eriksson's England turned Group 9 upside down with a historic 5–1 thrashing of Germany in their own Munich stronghold. Owen rampaged his way to a hat-trick which topped off what an admiring Franz Beckenbauer described as "the best football I have ever seen England play."

It wasn't all over yet. England unconvincingly beat Albania 2–0 at Newcastle to move to the top of the group, on goal difference, but almost came to grief against Greece at Old Trafford on the last matchday. Twice behind, a wonderful free kick from the magisterial Beckham in the last minute of added time delivered the 2–2 draw which – combined with Germany's simultaneous failure to beat Finland – edged England to the finals.

England, for all their football tradition and aura as home of the game, have won the

LOOK OUT FOR

DAVID BECKHAM

Position: Midfield *Club:* Manchester Utd
Previous club: Preston (on loan)
Born: 2 May 1975 *Intl apps:* 47 *Intl goals:* 6

The perception of David Beckham has turned full circle since he flew home in disgrace from the 1998 World Cup finals after being sent off in England's second-round defeat by Argentina. Then he was considered a bundle of petulance. But marriage to Victoria "Posh Spice" Adams, becoming a father and then captain of England have turned the target of abuse into the English football icon of his era. Beckham played a key role in Manchester United's European and domestic triumphs then topped it all with the inspired performance – and free-kick equaliser — which edged England past Greece and into the World Cup finals once more.

Below: David Beckham (7) strikes the crucial free-kick which equalized against Greece at Old Trafford last October and sent England into the World Cup finals as group winners.

World Cup only once: back in 1966. They will take a formidable weight of expectation with them to Korea and Japan.

Group F

NIGERIA
Will it be third time lucky?

Nigeria were, in 1998, the first African nation talked about in terms of potential World Cup winners. They were outsiders but, as Olympic champions, they demanded respect previously denied African contenders.

Sadly, a highly-talented squad disappointed. They opened with a dramatic 3–2 victory over Spain in which Sunday Oliseh struck a memorable winner then beat Bulgaria 1–0 to finish top of the group despite losing 3–1 to Paraguay. The second round saw Nigeria's dream end as they crashed 4-1 to Denmark. Thus they failed to emulate their 1994 finals debut when they also reached the second round before losing narrowly to Italy.

Nigeria approach the finals boasting the most talented squad of all the African contenders. Ike Shorunmu from Turkish club Besiktas has succeeded veteran Peter Rufai in goal with the defence ahead of him marshalled by the redoubtable Taribo West, a young veteran of top-level football in Italy,

England and Germany, and Chelsea's Celestine Babayaro.

Jay-Jay Okocha (Paris Saint-Germain) and Sunday Oliseh (Borussia Dortmund) are two of the finest midfield anchors operating in the world game, turning defence rapidly into attack with the assistance of Tijani Babangida and Finidi George (Ipswich), two sharp wingers. The goals are provided by Victor Agali (Schalke), Nwankwo Kanu (Arsenal) and new young talent Julius Aghahowa (Shakhtar Donetsk).

Close shave

Agali was Nigeria's leading scorer in the qualifying series with four goals including the first in the conclusive and crucial 3–0 destruction of Ghana as they came back from the brink of elimination to secure a third consecutive appearance in the finals. They had beaten Eritrea easily enough, 4-0 on aggregate, in the first round. But for much of the group phase it looked as if Nigeria would be edged out by George Weah's Liberia.

Nigeria did not help their own cause with a string of poor performances provoked by internal bickering which ultimately provoked the departure of coach Jo Bonfrere, the Dutchman in charge of the 1996 Olympic team. Shuaibu Amodu duly returned for yet another successful stint as caretaker manager.

A 1–0 defeat by Sierra Leone in Freetown spelled the end of the road for Bonfrere. That left Amodu with three matches in which to stage a highly convincing rescue act. First Liberia were beaten 2–0 then came a 4–0 win away to Sudan.

Nigeria have all the credentials to go a long way in South Korea and Japan. Apart from being Africa's first Olympic football champions in 1996, they won the FIFA World Under-17 Cup in 1985 and 1993 and lifted the African Nations Cup in 1994 and 2000.

Four years ago Michel Platini tipped Nigeria to go further than any previous African team at the World Cup. In the event, they let him down. On the other hand, perhaps his suggestion was just four years ahead of its time.

World Cup Record

1930	did not enter	1970	did not qualify
1934	did not enter	1974	disqualified
1938	did not enter	1978	did not qualify
1950	did not enter	1982	did not qualify
1954	did not enter	1986	did not qualify
1958	did not enter	1990	did not qualify
1962	did not qualify	1994	finals 2nd round
1966	withdrew	1998	finals 2nd round

The Coach

Amodu Shaibu *Career:* Played for Niger Tornadoes; Coach of BCC Lions, Shooting Stars Ibadan, Orlando Pirates (South Africa).
Born: 18 April 1960 *Appointed:* May 2001

Star Performers

Sunday Oliseh *Position:* Midfield *Club:* Borussia Dortmund (Germany) *Born:* 14 January 1974
Taribo West *Position:* Defender *Club:* Kaiserslautern (Germany) *Born:* 26 March 1974
Jay Jay Okocha *Position:* Midfield *Club:* Paris St Germain (France) *Born:* 14 August 1973
Finidi George *Position:* Striker *Club:* Ipswich Town (England) *Born:* 15 April 1971
Victor Agali *Position:* Striker *Club:* Schalke 04 *Born:* 29 December 1978

The Road to the Finals

Eritrea 0–0 Nigeria	Ghana 0–0 Nigeria
Nigeria 4–0 Eritrea	Sierra Leone 1–0 Nigeria
Nigeria 2–0 Sierra Leone	Nigeria 2–0 Liberia
Liberia 2–1 Nigeria	Sudan 0–4 Nigeria
Nigeria 3–0 Sudan	Nigeria 3–0 Ghana

Jay Jay Okocha (10) scores the equalizer for Nigeria in the 2000 African Cup of Nations Final against Cameroon.

Group F

Henrik Larsson drives in a free kick in the 3–0 win over Azerbaijan in Sweden's final qualifying game.

SWEDEN

Looking for a fifth top-four finish

In 1998–99, Sweden had the best record in the European Championship qualifiers, but were a huge disappointment in the finals. Having emulated the first part of the feat in the World Cup 2002 qualifiers, Sweden will be out to prove they can compete with the best the world can offer.

Sweden were one of no fewer than eight nations who cruised unbeaten through the mini-leagues stage of the European qualifying tournament. But none of the other seven – Croatia, Denmark, Italy, Portugal, Republic of Ireland, Slovenia and Spain – boasted as many as 26 points. Tommy Soderberg's men won eight of their 10 matches and were held 1–1, by Turkey in Gothenburg, and 0–0, by Slovakia in Bratislava.

The Swedes have a fine tradition for raising their game when it comes to the World Cup, finishing fourth in 1938 and 1994, third in 1950 and runners-up as hosts in 1958. The 1994 squad finished third by doing the simple things effectively, solid goalkeeping from Tomas Ravelli, perceptive midfield control from Jonas Thern and Stefan Schwarz, plus the attacking skills of Tomas Brolin.

Fringe players then – such as Celtic striker Henrik Larsson – have graduated now to senior status. He was Sweden's eight-goal top scorer in the qualifying event, with four in the 6–0 win over Moldova.

Continental drift

In 1958 Sweden relied heavily on their exiled talent and in 2000–01 only four squad regulars in the qualifying tournament played for Swedish clubs – the sort of imbalance which, as Soderberg and assistant Lars Lagerback pointed out, had not harmed France in 1998.

Adding to the confusion for opponents, Sweden fielded no fewer than five players named Andersson (defenders Patrik and Christoffer, midfielders Daniel Jerry and Anders plus striker Andreas) and four named Svensson (defender Michael, midfielders Anders and Magnus and forward Matthias).

Soderberg replaced Tommy Svensson as national manager in the autumn of 1997 after Sweden's disappointing failure to qualify for the 1998 World Cup finals. He and Lagerback took Sweden to the finals of Euro 2000 but they were eliminated in the first round – losing 2–1 to both Belgium and Italy and drawing 0–0 with Turkey.

Pressure began to build up on the managerial duo when the Swedes collected only five points and two goals from their opening three matches in the World Cup qualifiers – a scrambled 1–0 win in Azerbaijan, and the draws with Turkey and Slovakia. A 1–0 defeat of FYR Macedonia in Gothenburg in March 2001 proved the turning point. Andreas Svensson snatched the decisive goal just before half-time.

In spring 2001 Swedish football became the international vogue as Patrik Andersson anchored Bayern Munich's Champions League-winning defence and Larsson waltzed away with the golden boot awarded to European's leading league marksman after his 35-goal extravaganza in Scotland.

ITALY
Searching for a fourth World Cup

Group G

World Cup Record			
1930	did not enter	**1970**	runners-up
1934	winners	**1974**	finals 1st round
1938	winners	**1978**	fourth place
1950	finals 1st round	**1982**	winners
1954	finals 1st round	**1986**	finals 2nd round
1958	failed to qualify	**1990**	third place
1962	finals 1st round	**1994**	runners-up
1966	finals 1st round	**1998**	quarter-final

The Coach

Giovanni Trappattoni *Career:* Played for Milan, Italian national team, Coach of Milan, Juventus, Internazionale, Bayern Munich (Germany), Cagliari, Fiorentina *Born:* 17 March 1939 *Appointed:* August 2000

Star Performers

Francesco Totti *Position:* Striker
Club: Roma *Born:* 27 September 1976
Alessandro Del Piero *Position:* Striker
Club: Juventus *Born:* 9 September 1974
Fabio Cannavaro *Position:* Central defender
Club: Parma *Born:* 13 September 1973
Filippo Inzaghi *Position:* Striker
Club: Internazionale *Born:* 12 July 1973
Gianluigi Buffon *Position:* Goalkeeper
Club: Juventus *Born:* 28 January 1978

The Road to the Finals

Hungary 2–2 Italy	Italy 4–0 Lithuania
Italy 3–0 Romania	Georgia 1–2 Italy
Italy 2–0 Georgia	Lithuania 0–0 Italy
Romania 0–2 Italy	Italy 1–0 Hungary

Celebration time again for Italy's Luigi Di Biagio (14), Francesco Totti (20) and Marco Delvecchio after the latter had scored in the Euro 2000 Final in Rotterdam.

Italy's belief in a virtual divine right to win the World Cup has proved more of a hindrance than a help to a succession both of managers and of some of the finest players in European football history. But the Azzurri's record stands comparison with the finest in Europe.

Italy were the first nation in Europe to host the finals, then the first to host the finals twice. They were the first European nation to win the World Cup, the first ever to win it twice, as well as the first European nation to win the game's greatest prize three times.

There have been embarrassing exits and failures too, but these go back more than three decades. Indeed, Italy's record of five top-four finishes since 1970 is matched by Brazil and Germany, but not bettered. In fact, Italy last lost a World Cup knock-out match in 1986, going down on penalties in 1990 (in the semi-final to Argentina), 1994 (in the Final against Brazil) and 1998 (against eventual winners France in the quarter-finals).

In recent decades, the World Cup has provided more glory than the European Championships, at least until 2000, when Italy surprised many experts by reaching the Final. The task of shoring up fragile morale and providing an effective tactical framework has fallen to veteran coach Giovanni Trapattoni who succeeded Dino Zoff after Italy's painful golden goal defeat by France in the Euro 2000 Final.

Easy qualification

Italy were never in danger in European qualifying group eight, though they teased their fans in the closing stages. The Italians opened with a 2–2 draw in Hungary then ran up successive wins over Romania (twice), Georgia (twice) and Lithuania.

Typically, on the brink of qualifying, Italy's nerves frayed. Guaranteed at least a place in the play-offs, they scrambled a goalless draw against bottom of the table Lithuania in Kaunas. A victory would have ensured automatic qualification.

THE COACH
GIOVANNI TRAPATTONI

Trapattoni played wing-half with AC Milan and Italy in the 1960s, reputedly the only man who could hold Pele by fair means rather than foul. As a coach Trapattoni won every club prize possible with Juventus and Bayern Munich. Also bossed Internazionale, Cagliari and Fiorentina. Took over Italy when Dino Zoff resigned surprisingly after Euro 2000.

Eventually it took a minimalist performance and 1–0 win over no-hopers Hungary to secure Italy's four-point advantage over Romania and ticket to the finals. Juventus' Alessandro Del Piero, from whom Italian fans have awaited so much for so long, scored the crucial goal right on half-time.

Trapattoni – who has won almost every major honour as a player and coach in club football – is blessed with an abundance of talent. Francesco Toldo and Gianluigi Buffon are two of Europe's sharpest goalkeepers, Alessandro Nesta and Fabio Cannavaro two of the world's finest centre-backs and skipper Paolo Maldini still the game's outstanding left-side defender or wing-back. Serie A, the domestic league, is full of disciplined playmakers from whom Trapattoni can take his pick while Del Piero and Roma's Francesco Totti are among the world's most creative forwards.

The trick, for Trapattoni, is the apparently simple one of getting the mixture right. But the magic spell can prove elusive. A string of high-profile predecessors have been sacked or resigned in the face of massive media criticism for waving the wand over the wrong players.

Cuauhtemoc Blanco, one of their heroes from the 1998 finals in France. He also created the other goal for Juan Francisco Palencia.

Victory represented not merely relief but triumph for coach and former World Cup midfielder Javier Aguirre. He had taken over an apparently sinking ship five months earlier after Mexico had been humiliated at the Confederations Cup in South Korea and Japan and lost 2–1 at home to Costa Rica and then 3–1 away to Honduras in the World Cup. Mexico had never before been beaten at home in the World Cup qualifiers nor had they been defeated in the Azteca since 1981.

World Cup Record

1930	finals 1st round	**1970**	finals 1st round
1934	did not enter	**1974**	did not qualify
1938	did not enter	**1978**	finals 1st round
1950	finals 1st round	**1982**	did not qualify
1954	finals 1st round	**1986**	quarter-finals
1958	finals 1st round	**1990**	suspended
1962	finals 1st round	**1994**	finals 2nd round
1966	finals 1st round	**1998**	finals 2nd round

The Coach

Javier Aguirre *Career:* Played for America, Atlante, Osasuna (Spain), Guadalajara Mexico national team; Coach of Atlante, Pachuca.
Born: 1 December 1958 *Appointed:* June 2001

Star Performers

Alberto Garcia Aspe *Position:* Midfield
Club: Puebla *Born:* 11 May 1967
Miguel Zepeda *Position:* Defender
Club: Atlas *Born:* 25 May 1976
Claudio Suarez *Position:* Defender
Club: Tigres *Born:* 17 December 1968
Juan Francisco Palencia *Position:* Forward
Club: Espanyol (Spain) *Born:* 28 April 1973
Oscar Perez *Position:* Goalkeeper
Club: Cruz Azul *Born:* 1 February 1973

The Road to the Finals

Panama 0–1 Mexico
Trinidad & Tobago 1–0 Mexico
Mexico 2–0 Canada
Mexico 7–1 Panama
Mexico 7–0 Trinidad & Tobago
Canada 0–0 Mexico
United States 2–0 Mexico
Mexico 4–0 Jamaica
Trinidad & Tobago 1–1 Mexico
Mexico 1–2 Costa Rica
Honduras 3–1 Mexico
Mexico 1–0 United States
Jamaica 1–2 Mexico
Mexico 3–0 Trinidad & Tobago
Costa Rica 0–0 Mexico
Mexico 3–0 Honduras

Luis Hernandez (right) wins this tussle with Carlos Castro, but Mexico lost last June's World Cup qualifying tie against Costa Rica in Mexico City 2–1.

Group G

MEXICO
Capable of upsetting the best

Long gone are the days when Mexico strolled through, unchallenged, to the World Cup finals from the Central and North American and Caribbean qualifying section. They remain a power in the region but no longer does their intimidating reputation carry the same weight. Proof was evident in the manner of Mexico's access to the 2002 finals.

Three places were available to the six nations in the concluding qualifying group and Costa Rica and the United States had grabbed two of them before the last matchday. The remaining place was between Mexico and Honduras who faced each other level on points. Mexico had the better goal difference and thus needed only a draw to qualify. In the event they won 3–0 with two goals from

CUAUHTEMOC BLANCO

Position: Forward *Club:* Valladolid (Sp)
Previous clubs: America, Necaxa, America
Born: 17 January 1973 *Intl apps:* 46 *Intl goals:* 18

Cuauhtemoc Blanco was outstanding at France 98, his pace, shooting and self-confidence lifting Mexico to victory over South Korea, dramatic draws against Belgium and Holland and a narrow second-round defeat by Germany. Now Blanco had a worldwide reputation to add to the regional renown he had secured in 1996 by helping Mexico win the CONCACAF Gold Cup and the US Cup. Blanco then played for top outfit America, but his subsequent transfer to Necaxa propelled his new club to CONCACAF Champions Cup success and on to third place in the FIFA Club World Championship in 2000. He was Mexico's eight-goal top scorer in the 2002 qualifiers.

Cuauhtemoc Blanco of Mexico wheels away in delight after scoring one of his two goals against Honduras in the 3–0 victory in Mexico City last November; he scored eight goals in the qualifying competition.

Back from the abyss

The Mexicans had thus sunk to fifth in the six-nation group when Aguirre replaced Enrique Meza. A place in the finals appeared almost beyond reach. Fortunately, Aguirre was able to welcome back Blanco after a lengthy injury absence. His first match in charge was against the USA. A lone goal after 15 minutes from Jared Francisco Borguetti decided it in Mexico's favour and turned team spirit around.

Two goals from Blanco earned victory in Jamaica and he scored another in a home beating of Trinidad & Tobago. A goalless draw away to leaders Costa Rica set up the Mexicans for the decisive dismissal of Honduras.

Mexico's best World Cups were in 1970 and 1986, when they were hosts. They reached the quarter-finals of both and in 1986 were unlucky to lose on penalties to West Germany. In 1998 the Mexicans ended the first round unbeaten after a 3–1 victory over South Korea and 2–2 draws against Belgium and Holland. Disappointingly, they

lost 2–1 to Germany in the second round. But Mexican fans are tired of hearing about history. They are impatient for their favourites to make an impression at the World Cup finals.

Goalkeeper Oscar Perez, veteran defender Claudio Suarez, playmaker Alberto Garcia Aspe and forwards Palencia and Jesus Arellano survive from the 1998 squad. Most important, so does Blanco. Aguirre and all of Mexico will look to him in Korea and Japan.

JAVIER AGUIRRE

Aguirre made his World Cup finals debut as a midfielder when hosts Mexico reached the quarter-finals in 1986. Played for America, Atlante, Osasuna (Spain) and Guadalajara then coached Pachuca to their surprise 1999 championship win. Became national boss when Mexico appeared on the brink of elimination in the World Cup qualifiers.

CROATIA

Capable of causing a surprise

Group G

World Cup Record

1930	did not enter	**1970**	did not enter
1934	did not enter	**1974**	did not enter
1938	did not enter	**1978**	did not enter
1950	did not enter	**1982**	did not enter
1954	did not enter	**1986**	did not enter
1958	did not enter	**1990**	did not enter
1962	did not enter	**1994**	did not enter
1966	did not enter	**1998**	third place

The Coach

Mirko Jozic
Career: Coach of FC Junak (Yugoslavia), Yugoslavia national youth team, Colo-Colo (Chile), Chile national team, America (Mexico) Hajduk Splilt, Al Hilal (Saudi Arabia), Newell's Old Boys (Argentina), Sporting Lisbon (Portugal), .
Born: 8 April 1940 *Appointed:* November 2000

Star Performers

Igor Tudor *Position:* Defender
Club: Juventus (Italy) *Born:* 16 April 1978
Alen Boksic *Position:* Striker
Club: Middlesbrough (England) *Born:* 31 January 1970
Robert Jarni *Position:* Midfield
Club: Las Palmas (Spain) *Born:* 26 October 1968
Dario Stimac *Position:* Defender
Club: Internazionale (Italy) *Born:* 12 November 1975
Goran Vlaovic *Position:* Striker
Club: Panathinaikos (Greece) *Born:* 7 August 1972

The Road to the Finals

Belgium 0–0 Croatia	Latvia 0–1 Croatia
Croatia 1–1 Scotland	Scotland 0–0 Croatia
Croatia 4–1 Latvia	San Marino 0–4 Croatia
Croatia 4–0 San Marino	Croatia 1–0 Belgium

Alen Boksic has been one of Croatia's stalwarts in their rush to join the world game's premier league.

Croatia boast a remarkable World Cup record: one appearance at the finals and the reward of the bronze medals for finishing third. That was in France four years ago – though they were not, in fact, total newcomers to international football.

The country existed as an independent political – and thus football – entity, albeit under puppet regime conditions, in the 1940s. The Croats organized their own league championship and their own national team. But, under direction from Berlin, they played against only other Axis-aligned nations Germany, Italy, Bulgaria and Romania.

Croatia remained a significant source of football strength and talent within the former Yugoslavia after the war. Dinamo Zagreb – briefly known as FC Croatia – and Hajduk Split built impressive records in European club competitions, which they have extended since Croatia's independent re-emergence in 1990.

The first match of the new era was a 2–1 win over the United States on 17 October 1990 and the nucleus of that team reached the Euro 96 quarter-finals, in their first appearance on the major international stage.

Experience tells

Outstanding players included striker Davor Suker, as well as playmakers Zvonimir Boban and Robert Prosinecki who had played for Yugoslavia at the 1990 World Cup finals. All three had been World Youth Cup winners with the former Yugoslavia in 1987 and they maintained their prowess at senior World Cup level in 1998.

Not only did Croatia finish third but also Suker collected the golden boot as the event's six-goal leading marksman. He scored in every round including the semi-final in which Croatia lost 2–1 to France and the third place play-off in which they beat Holland 2–1.

Fans worried about Croatia's old favourites having gone over the hill when they opened the 2002 qualifying series with draws away to Belgium and home to Scotland. Approaching the climactic rounds of the group, Belgium were group favourites with Croatia and Scotland duelling for the runners-up spot.

But strikers Goran Vlaovic and Alen Boksic recovered fitness and form while a new attacking hero emerged in Bosko Balaban. They went into the last matchday in second place above Scotland, but two points behind Belgium – who were the visitors to Zagreb.

Prosinecki fluffed a penalty, but substitute Balaban laid on a goal for Boksic 14 minutes from time for Croatia to top the group and qualify for the finals for the second successive time. For national coach Mirko Jozic the international wheel had turned full circle: he was boss of the juniors who had won the World Youth Cup for the former Yugoslavia 15 years ago.

Jozic had worked effectively since being appointed in December 2000 to succeed Miroslav Blazevic, the veteran coach who had put together the initial Croatia squad. Jozic has mixed the "old guard" with newer talents such as goalkeeper Stipe Pletikosa, brothers Nico and Robert Kovac, plus attacking talent Balaban.

Group G

ECUADOR
Newcomers to the party

Ecuador – after near misses in qualifying for the 1966 and 1998 tournaments – are one of four newcomers at the 2002 World Cup finals. Their surprise success means that Venezuela are now the only CONMEBOL (South American Confederation) country never to have appeared at the pinnacle of the world game.

Coming into the 2002 qualifiers, Ecuador hardly appeared to offer a great threat to the traditional giants of the region. They had never won the Copa America and no Ecuador club had ever won the Copa Libertadores, the continent's club championship. The best they could boast was a runners-up performance from top club Barcelona of Guayaquil in 1990.

It is a measure of Ecuador's place in the international shadows that, compared with most of their South American rivals in the qualifiers, only a handful of their players had to be recalled for national service from foreign clubs.

Two were in defence in commander Ivan Hurtado (Tigres, Mexico) and rightback Ulises de la Cruz (Hibernian, Scotland). Up front Ivan Kaviedes starred with Celta Vigo in Spain while top scorer Agustin Delgado was transferred after the qualifying campaign – despite knee trouble – from Mexico's Necaxa to England's Southampton.

The federation's increased ambition became evident in the late 1990s when Francisco Maturana, former World Cup finals boss of Colombia, was appointed national coach. He quit after the 1998 qualifying failure before the federation turned to his former assistant, Hernan Dario Gomez.

Head for heights

A second key decision by the federation was to ignore the pressure from the likes of Argentina and Brazil and play all their home matches at altitude in Quito. The decision paid off immediately handsomely. Ecuador won six of their nine home games, collecting 20 of their 31 total points in Quito.

By the time they lost at home to Argentina in August 2001, the impossible dream of a place in the World Cup finals was in sight. A 1–1 draw against Uruguay meant Ecuador

had secured their ticket for the finals in Korea and Japan with one game to play.

Drama was not restricted only to the pitch. Ecuador's campaign was thrown in confusion halfway through when coach Gomez was beaten up and shot in the leg by an angry fan bearing a grudge over Gomez's team selection for the World Youth Cup in Argentina. Gomez, on his release from hospital, quit his job and flew home to Colombia.

His players were devastated. Several threatened to quit the national team unless the federation persuaded Gomez to return. In the end it took a personal plea from Hurtado and playmaker Alex Aguinaga, who flew to Colombia, before Gomez agreed to change his mind.

Ecuador's subsequent achievement in reaching the finals duly rewarded not only his own work but justified the players' faith in their own manager.

World Cup Record

1930	did not enter	**1970**	did not qualify
1934	did not enter	**1974**	did not qualify
1938	did not enter	**1978**	did not qualify
1950	withdrew	**1982**	did not qualify
1954	did not enter	**1986**	did not qualify
1958	did not enter	**1990**	did not qualify
1962	did not qualify	**1994**	did not qualify
1966	did not qualify	**1998**	did not qualify

The Coach

Hernan Dario Gomez *Career:* Played for Nacional Medellin (Colombia); Coach of Nacional Medellin (Colombia), Colombia national team, *Born:* 3 February 1956 *Appointed:* August 1999

Star Performers

Ivan Hurtado *Position:* Defender
Club: Tigres (Mexico) Born: 16 August 1974
Ulises de la Cruz *Position:* Defender
Club: Hibernian (Scotland) Born: 8 February 1974
Agustin Delgado *Position:* Forward
Club: Southampton (England) Born: 23 December 1974
Ivan Kaviedes *Position:* Forward
Club: Celta Vigo (Spain) Born: 24 October 1977
Alex Aguinaga *Position:* Midfield
Club: Necaxa (Mexico) Born: 9 July 1968

The Road to the Finals

Ecuador 2–0 Venezuela	Venezuela 1–2 Ecuador
Brazil 3–2 Ecuador	Ecuador 1–0 Brazil
Paraguay 3–1 Ecuador	Ecuador 2–1 Paraguay
Ecuador 2–1 Peru	Peru 1–2 Ecuador
Argentina 2–0 Ecuador	Ecuador 0–2 Argentina
Ecuador 0–0 Colombia	Colombia 0–0 Ecuador
Ecuador 2–0 Bolivia	Bolivia 1–5 Ecuador
Uruguay 4–0 Ecuador	Ecuador 1–1 Uruguay
Ecuador 1–0 Chile	Chile 0–0 Ecuador

Cleber Chala (16) narrowly evades a wild Paraguayan tackle on Ecuador's way to the finals.

63

Group H

JAPAN
Joint hosts want first finals victory

World Cup Record

1930	did not enter	**1970**	did not qualify
1934	did not enter	**1974**	did not qualify
1938	withdrew	**1978**	did not qualify
1950	did not enter	**1982**	did not qualify
1954	did not quality	**1986**	did not qualify
1958	did not enter	**1990**	did not qualify
1962	did not qualify	**1994**	did not qualify
1966	did not enter	**1998**	finals 1st round

The Coach

Philippe Troussier *Career:* Played for Angouleme, Red Star Paris, Rouen, Reims (all France). Coach of Red Star Paris, Cretail (both France), Kaizer Chiefs, Orlando Pirates (both South Africa), ASEC Abidjan (Côte d'Ivoire), Côte d'Ivoire, Nigeria, Burkina Faso, South Africa. *Born:* 21 March 1955 *Appointed:* September 1998

Star Performers

Hiroaki Morishima *Position:* Midfielder
Club: Cerezo Osaka *Born:* 30 April 1972
Akinori Nishizawa *Position:* Striker
Club: Bolton Wanderers (England) *Born:* 18 June 1976
Shinji Ono *Position:* Midfielder
Club: Feyenoord (Holland) *Born:* 27 September 1979
Yoshikatsu Kawaguchi *Position:* Goalkeeper
Club: Portsmouth (England) *Born:* 15 August 1977
Junichi Inamoto *Position:* Defender
Club: Arsenal (England) *Born:* 18 September 1979

The Road to the Finals

Qualified automatically as hosts

Shigeyoshi Mochizuki leaves behind Mohammad Al Shalhoub of Saudi Arabia during Japan's 2000 Asian Cup Final victory in Beirut, Lebanon.

JAPAN have dreamed of hosting the World Cup finals ever since Sir Stanley Rous, then president of FIFA, first suggested the idea back in the mid-1960s. Sir Stanley recognized that this was no overnight project. Indeed, it took decades of hard work behind the scenes inspired by the ambition of the Japanese Football Association.

First Japan became home for the annual World Club Cup, then full-time professional football was introduced followed by the launch of the J.League in 1993. The newly-created corporate-backed teams used their wealth to attract numerous star veterans including England's Gary Lineker, Brazil's Dunga, Leonardo and Zico, Italy's Toto Schillaci and Germany's Guido Buchwald and Pierre Littbarski.

Simultaneously, the Japanese put together an impressive bid for the hosting rights to the 2002 World Cup. Japan undoubtedly had the stadiums, communications and facilities to stage the event alone but, ultimately, political considerations within FIFA meant they were assigned to share host rights with South Korea.

Late, aggressive South Korean intrusion meant the 2002 competition is shared but, at least, Japan will stage Asia's first World Cup Final – in Yokohama. And Japan is the Asian team most likely to make finals life awkward for the visiting elite from Europe and South America.

Japan almost qualified for the finals for the first time in 1994. Going into the final game of the qualifying tournament they needed a victory to reach the United States but Japan conceded a last minute goal against Iraq and missed qualification.

Finals debut

No such mistake was made next time around. Japan not only reached the finals in France but gave a hard-working account of themselves

Hidetoshi Nakata takes on the Brazil defence during Japan's 0–0 draw in the 2001 Confederations Cup at the Kashima Stadium in Ibaraki.

despite losing all three matches. They fell by the minimum 1–0 against Argentina and Croatia and then by 2–1 against Jamaica. Masashi Nakayama had the honour of scoring Japan's first goal in the finals.

Media speculation suggested that the JFA wanted Arsène Wenger to lead them into the 2002 World Cup. But he was contracted to Arsenal so they turned, instead, to fellow Frenchman Philippe Troussier who had coached South Africa at the 1998 finals.

Troussier came under increasing pressure after disappointing results in friendlies but then turned the corner after guiding Japan to victory in the 2000 Asian Cup in Lebanon. Key man for Japan is Italian-based midfielder Hidetoshi Nakata. He was outstanding at France 98 and his success in Serie A with Perugia, Roma and Parma has enhanced his superstar status back home. His progress became all the more important after injuries upset the development of equally talented Hiroshi Nanami, Japan's free-kick expert.

Up front, Japan hope Feyenoord's Shinji Ono and Bolton's Akinori Nishizawa have learned plenty from their time in Europe because they need an effective marksman to fill the gap left by the fading of Kazu Miura, Japan's first modern superstar. Whoever achieves that goal will earn a place in Japanese football legend.

THE COACH

PHILIPPE TROUSSIER

Frenchman who built his coaching reputation in Africa. Had successful club stints with ASEC (Ivory Coast), Kaizer Chiefs (South Africa) and FAS (Morocco) and coached the national teams of Ivory Coast, Nigeria and Burkina Faso before managing South Africa on their World Cup debut in 1998. Guided Japan to their Asian Cup triumph in 2000.

LOOK OUT FOR

HIDETOSHI NAKATA

Position: Midfield *Club:* Parma (It)
Previous clubs: Shonan Bellmare, Perugia (It), Roma (It)
Born: 22 January 1977 *Intl apps:* 49 *Intl goals:* 11

Midfield dynamo Hidetoshi Nakata was not the first Japanese export to Italian football – that honour belonged to Kaziu Miura – but he has been far more successful. Perugia gambled on him after being impressed by the way Nakata inspired Japan to reach the World Cup finals for the first time in 1998. His popularity with Japanese tourists earned millions of pounds for the local tourist industry, which was as disappointed as Perugia's fans when Nakata was sold to Roma in 2000. Failure to secure a regular first-team place upset his form – although he was part of Roma's championship-winning squad – and he was sold again, to Parma in July 2001, where he hoped to regain his confidence for the most crucial World Cup campaign in Japan's history.

failed to progress beyond the opening group round. The Russian effort had been hampered from the outset by all sorts of political and managerial problems and the national team was still regaining its pride and confidence after the collapse of the Soviet regime.

That political cataclysm had a major effect on the national team because Russian football was thrown back onto its own resources without being to draw on the skills and talents of Ukraine, Belarus and Georgia.

Back on track

No wonder it has taken almost 10 years to regain proper equilibrium. Now Russia will be a difficult challenge for anyone in the finals – with a team founded on a foreign-based nucleus of talented men such as sweeper Yuri Nikiforov, defensive anchor Victor Onopko, playmakers Alexander Mostovoi and Valeri Karpin and Vladimir Bestchastnikh, their seven-goal top scorer in qualifying.

Bestchastnikh set Russia off to a winning start with the decisive lone goal in their opening win away to Switzerland in Zurich. Oddly, considering their steady dismissal of

World Cup Record — Soviet Union 1930–1990

1930	did not enter	**1970**	quarter-final
1934	did not enter	**1974**	disqualified
1938	did not enter	**1978**	did not qualify
1950	did not enter	**1982**	finals 2nd round
1954	did not enter	**1986**	finals 2nd round
1958	quarter-final	**1990**	finals 1st round
1962	quarter-final	**1994**	finals 1st round
1966	fourth place	**1998**	did not qualify

The Coach

Oleg Romantsev *Career:* Played for Spartak Moscow, Soviet Union national team. Coach of Spartak Moscow *Born:* 4 January 1954 *Appointed:* August 1999

Star Performers

Yuri Nikiforov *Position:* Defender
Club: PSV Eindhoven (Holland) *Born:* 16 September 1970
Ruslan Nigmatullin *Position:* Goalkeeper
Club: Verona (Italy) *Born:* 7 October 1974
Valeri Karpin *Position:* Midfielder
Club: Celta Vigo (Spain) *Born:* 2 Feburary 1969
Alexander Mostovoi *Position:* Midfielder
Club: Celta Vigo (Spain) *Born:* 22 August 1968
Vladimir Bestchastnykh *Position:* Striker
Club: Spartak Moscow *Born:* 1 April 1974

Group H

RUSSIA
No substitute for experience

Russia could not choose a more appropriate setting than the World Cup finals in which to celebrate their 10th anniversary as an independent football nation.

Under the experienced guidance of Spartak Moscow supremo Oleg Romantsev, the Russians led European qualifying group one from start to finish – losing only one of their 10 games and that to runners-up Slovenia only after qualification was virtually assured.

The last time Russia appeared at the finals was in the United States in 1994 when, despite a 6–1 thrashing of Cameroon, they

The Road to the Finals

Switzerland 0–1 Russia	Russia 1–1 Yugoslavia
Russia 3–0 Luxembourg	Luxembourg 1–2 Russia
Russia 1–1 Slovenia	Slovenia 2–1 Russia
Russia 1–0 Faroe Islands	Faroe Islands 0–3 Russia
Yugoslavia 0–1 Russia	Russia 4–0 Switzerland

Vladimir Bestchastnykh was Russia's seven-goal leading scorer in qualifying for the 2002 World Cup finals.

everyone else, the Russians were held 1–1 at home by both Slovenia and Yugoslavia. But the ever-dangerous Bestchastnikh struck the winner away to Yugoslavia in Belgrade and then two more in the 3–0 away win over the Faroe Islands which ensured Russia topped the table.

Multi-nationals

Russia entered the Olympic Games in 1912 but the Communist revolution meant that for almost all of the 20th century, international football was by Soviet Union squads containing players from Russia, Ukraine, Georgia, Latvia, and all the other republics in the Union of Soviet Socialist Republics (USSR).

They enjoyed much success in the Olympic Games and European Championships, but the Soviet Union's World Cup record was surprisingly poor. After the communist collapse, the Soviet Union rematerialized as the Commonwealth of Independent States at the 1992 European Championship finals.

Months later the newly-independent Russian federation won the political battle to assume the Soviet Union's place in the international game. All the former players were offered the unique opportunity of representing any of the new national teams that were formed and a few non-Russians opted to play for the largest nation in the region. That 1994 team did set one World Cup finals record as Oleg Salenko scored five goals in the win over Cameroon

Many of those players have passed into retirement, so now it is up to their own players to justify Russia's place at the pinnacle of world football.

THE COACH

OLEG ROMANTSEV

Moscow-born Romantsev was originally a stalwart left-back with Spartak, winning 12 caps for the former Soviet Union, before graduating to club coach. Managed Russia in the 1996 European Championship while simultaneously establishing Spartak as virtual permanent national champions in his dual role as president and coach.

VIKTOR ONOPKO

Position: Central defence *Club:* Oviedo (Sp)
Previous clubs: Stakhanovets, Kiev Dynamo (Ukr), Shakhtyor Donetsk (Ukr), Moscow Spartak (Rus)
Born: 14 October 1969 *Intl apps:* 89 *Intl goals:* 6

Victor Onopko's consistency at the heart of defence was demonstrated by the fact that he played every minute of all 10 of Russia's qualifying ties (the only other player to do so being keeper Ruslan Nigmatullin). Originally Onopko was an attacking left-back when he emerged in the turbulent early 1990s – playing international football for the Soviet Union, then for the Commonwealth of Independent States in Euro 92 and finally for the newly-independent Russia in the 1994 World Cup. A former youth and under-21 international, Onopko made his senior debut in a 2–2 draw against England in 1992. Twice voted Russia's Footballer of the Year.

Victor Onopko (left) blocks a rare shot on goal from Luxembourg's Sascha Schneider during Russia's 2–1 away victory in last June's qualifying match.

Group H

BELGIUM
Red Devils on the upswing

The Coach

Robert Waseige *Career:* Played for FC Liège, Racing White Brussels, Winterslag; Coach of Winterslag, Sporting Lokeren, FC Liège, Charleroi, Standard Liège, Sporting Clube (Portugal), Charleroi.
Born: 26 August 1939 *Appointed:* August 1999

Star Performers

Marc Wilmots *Position:* Midfield
Club: Schalke 04 (Germany) *Born:* 22 February 1969
Emil Mpenza *Position:* Striker
Club: Schalke 04 (Germany) *Born:* 4 July 1978
Geert De Vlieger *Position:* Goalkeeper
Club: Willem II (Holland) *Born:* 16 October 1970
Eric Deflandre *Position:* Defender
Club: Olympique Lyonnais (France) *Born:* 2 August 1973
Gert Verheyen *Position:* Midfield
Club: Club Brugge *Born:* 20 September 1970

The Road to the Finals

Belgium 0–0 Croatia
Latvia 0–4 Belgium
Belgium 10–1 San Marino
Scotland 2–2 Belgium
Belgium 3–1 Latvia
San Marino 1–4 Belgium
Belgium 2–0 Scotland
Croatia 1–0 Belgium
Belgium 1–0 Czech Republic
Czech Republic 0–1 Belgium

Belgium goalkeeper Geert De Vlieger punches clear from Scotland's Don Hutchison during the 2–2 draw last June.

Belgian national team coach Robert Waseige has had two major challenges in his spell in charge. The first was to turn Belgium from a shambles into a reasonable team in time for the 2000 European Championship. His second was to turn his first-round failures on that occasion into World Cup finalists.

The national team, the so-called Red Devils was suffering from a depressing lack of hellfire spirit. Belgium had won only twice in 11 games, and had lost home friendlies to the Czech Republic, Bulgaria, Egypt and Finland. Georges Leekens, the coach who had taken Belgium to the 1998 World Cup finals, had lost the confidence of both fans and media.

Thus the Belgian federation turned to veteran coach Waseige who had just completed a stint with Charleroi. As technical committee chairman Karel Vertongen said: "He has all the right qualities. He has experience, wisdom, knowledge of the players – and he is available."

The inherent quality of Belgian football had never been in doubt. FIFA founding members in 1904, Belgium had been just one of four European nations to play in the inaugural competition and apart from 1950 – when they withdrew without playing a match – have played in every qualifying competition, and this is their 11th finals.

Top clubs Anderlecht and Brugge have long been powerful contenders in European competition while the national team were European Championship runners-up in 1980 and semi-finalists in 1972 – to say nothing of World Cup semi-finalists in 1986.

Solid nucleus of stars

Results under Waseige reflected that new spirit though co-hosts Belgium were eliminated in the first round of "their" European finals after a 2–0 defeat by Turkey. At least he had built a solid nucleus of a team for the World Cup even though the Belgians finished group runners-up to Croatia and qualified via the play-off option, defeating the Czech Republic 1–0 both home and away.

Key man in midfield remains the long-striding Marc Wilmots. The Schalke general, a veteran of Belgium's 1994 and 1998 finals campaigns, also scored the all-important away goal against the Czechs in the second leg of the play-off in Prague. In attack Waseige has been delighted to welcome aboard Croatia-born striker Branko Strupar and the temperamental, Germany-based Emile Mpenza.

How Belgium fare in South Korea and Japan will decide how the likes of Wilmots, Mpenza and Co rank, ultimately, by comparison with heroes of the past such as 1930s forward Raymond Braine and top club Anderlecht's 1960s superstar Paul Van Himst.

Waseige appears to have revived the spirit of '86 in his present team – no more obviously then when they climbed back from 2–0 down, and with only 10 men, to force a 2–2 draw away to Scotland. That match, more than any other, proved the turning point which justified all Waseige's hard work.

Group H

TUNISIA
Wanting to prove a point

Tunisia fell in the first round of the finals in 1978 in Argentina and then again in France in 1998. They believe their talent and history deserve better and that they can prove the point in South Korea and Japan.

At least they went about the first stage of the challenge in workmanlike style, remaining undefeated in all 10 of their qualifying ties – starting with the comfortable 5–1 aggregate victory over Mauritania in the first round.

Tunisia's national team are more independently representative of their own football than any of the other four African finalists. The vast majority of both squad and likely starting line-up come from domestic clubs such as Esperance of Tunis, one of the most powerful outfits in the entire continent.

The national team, however, achieved qualifying success under foreign guidance. They launched their campaign under Italian coach Francesco Scoglio and concluded it under the well-travelled German manager, Eckhard Krautzun. But after qualification, Krautzun was also replaced, by Henri Michel.

A star player at Nantes and a French international, Michel coached France to the Olympic gold medal in 1984, World Cup third place two years later, and was at France 98 with Morocco.

Safety first

The coaching changes made little difference to a cautious tactical approach during qualification which saw Tunisia only ever daring play with two all-out attackers. That laid a heavy burden on the midfield players both to shut down the opposition's creative stars and provide as much support as possible for their own forwards.

Outstanding in this role was Zoubeir Beya, a right-sided midfielder or winger. Beya, one of the few foreign-based players, from Turkish club Besiktas, was Tunisia's top goalscorer in the qualifiers with six, including two in the concluding 3–0 win away to the Democratic Republic of Congo with which Tunisia secured their ticket to Korea and Japan.

Tunisia count among the aristocrats of African football. They were the second

African nation to reach the final rounds of the Olympic Games (in Rome in 1960) and were among the earliest and most enthusiastic supporters of both the African club cups and the Nations Cup – finishing runners-up in 1965 to Ghana and in 1996 to South Africa.

Their first star player was 1965 Nations Cup hero Majid Chetali. He re-emerged on the international stage in 1978 when he guided Tunisia to the World Cup finals in Argentina. Four successive qualifying failures followed before Tunisia returned to the finals in France where they lost to both England and Colombia before returning home with at least a little honour restored thanks to a consolation 1–1 draw with Romania.

Goalkeeper Chokri El-Ouer, defenders Khaled Badra, Sami Trabelsi and Tarek Thabet, midfielder Sirajedine Chihi and Beya were all in France and intend to put the lessons learned into practice in Korea and Japan.

World Cup Record

1930	did not enter	1970	did not qualify
1934	did not enter	1974	did not qualify
1938	did not enter	1978	finals 1st round
1950	did not enter	1982	did not qualify
1954	did not enter	1986	did not qualify
1958	did not enter	1990	did not qualify
1962	did not qualify	1994	did not qualify
1966	withdrew	1998	finals 1st round

The Coach

Henri Michel *Career:* Played for Nantes (France), France. Coach of France, PSG (France), Cameroon, Al Nasr (Saudi Arabia), Morocco, UAE, Salonika (Greece). *Born:* 28 October 1947 *Appointed:* November 2001

Star Performers

Zoubeir Beya *Position:* Midfield
Club: Besiktas (Turkey) *Born:* 15 May 1971
Chokri El-Ouer *Position:* Goalkeeper
Club: Esperance *Born:* 15 August 1976
Sirejeddine Chihi *Position:* Midfield
Club: Esperance *Born:* 16 April 1970
Sami Trabelsi *Position:* Defender
Club: Club Sfaxien *Born:* 4 February 1968
Ali Zitouni *Position:* Striker
Club: Esperance *Born:* 11 January 1981

The Road to the Finals

Mauritania 1–2 Tunisia
Tunisia 3–0 Mauritania
Côte d'Ivoire 2–2 Tunisia
Tunisia 1–0 Madagascar
Congo 1–2 Tunisia
Tunisia 6–0 Congo DR
Madagascar 0–2 Tunisia
Tunisia 1–1 Côte d'Ivoire
Tunisia 6–0 Congo
Congo DR 0–3 Tunisia

Goalkeeper Chokri El-Ouer is at full stretch to defy Egypt in the 2000 African Cup of Nations.

WORLD CUP HISTORY

From Trello Abegglen to Dino Zoff, the World Cup has been the ultimate stage for footballers to shine. FIFA did not award a player of the tournament until relatively recently, but almost every competition has been won by a country with one player who stood taller than all others when it really mattered.

The world's richest and most prestigious sports event, attracted a crowd of only 1,000 for its launch 72 years ago in Uruguay. But the concept of a world championship had been first raised 26 years earlier when FIFA was founded. At the time, most teams were amateurs and the Olympic Games winners were considered unofficial world champions. In 1924 and 1928 that meant Uruguay. But, as professional swept through European and South American football, FIFA recognised it was time to make the World Cup dream a reality. At its 1928 congress, the president, Jules Rimet, and the general-secretary of the French Football Association, Henri Delaunay, proposed a tournament every four years. The inaugural venue was decided at the following year's congress, one year ahead of the event. Italy, Holland, Spain and Sweden all applied to stage the first finals but withdrew in favour of Uruguay. Not only did the Uruguayans propose to celebrate 100 years of independence by welcoming the world and building a new 93,000-capacity stadium, they also offered to pay everyone's travel and hotel expenses.

Uruguay's Pablo Dorado strikes the opening goal against Argentina in the first World Cup Final in Montevideo in 1930.

1930
URUGUAY

The first finals were hardly representative of the world because of the 13 competing countries, four were European, seven came from the host continent, South America, plus the USA and Mexico. They were split into four groups with Uruguay, Argentina, Brazil and the United States the seeded nations. The four group winners advanced to the semi-finals. France beat Mexico 4–1 in the first World Cup match on July 13 before a meagre 1,000 spectators with Lucien Laurent scoring the historic opening goal. Argentina won the group and went on to thrash the USA 6–1 in the semi-finals. Uruguay beat Yugoslavia – 2–1 conquerors of Brazil – by the same margin in the other semi. The Final was a repeat of the 1928 Olympic final. Tension was so high that all spectators were searched for firearms on their way into the stadium. Argentina led 2–1 at half-time, but Uruguay hit back to win 4–2 – with goals from Dorado, Cea, Iriarte and Castro.

JOSÉ NASAZZI
URUGUAY

Born: 24 May 1901 **Position:** Right-back

José Nasazzi was the first captain ever to lift the World Cup trophy. Uruguay built their teams from the back and their best defender was right-back and skipper Nasazzi. Nicknamed "The Marshall", he had led Uruguay to victory in the 1928 Olympic Games and was a key player in the Naçional club side which dominated the domestic scene in Uruguay.

1934
ITALY

Italy emulated Uruguay – who stayed away in protest because only four European nations had taken part in the 1930 competition – by winning as hosts. Some 32 nations entered and a qualifying competition was necessary. This time the format was a simple knock-out event rather than mini-

GIANPIERO COMBI
ITALY

Born: 18 December 1902 **Position:** Goalkeeper

Gianpiero Combi (1934) and Dino Zoff (1982) had much in common. Both were goalkeepers for Juventus and Italy, both celebrated winning Lo Scudetto – the Italian league title – before winning the World Cup, and both captained the Azzuri. Combi played his entire career for Juventus, making his debut in 1923 winning six league championships, including five in a row 1931–35. He played 47 times for Italy.

leagues. This meant that first-round losers including Brazil, Argentina and the USA all went home after just one game – an 8,000-mile round trip for just 90 minutes' football. Italy underlined their status as the best team in the competition by defeating Austria's so-called "Wunderteam" 1–0 in the semi-finals. Czechoslovakia proved tough opposition in the Final. With eight minutes remaining they led 1–0 and it took a freakish goal from Raimundo Orsi to pull Italy level and earn extra time. Veteran centre-forward Angelo Schiavio scored the winner in extra time.

Opposite: *History in the making as captains Giuseppe Meazza (Italy) and Gyorgy Sarosi (Hungary) greet each other, and referee Pierre Capdeville, before the 1938 World Cup Final at the Stade de Colombes in Paris, won 4–2 by Italy.*

1938
FRANCE

By the time of the 1938 finals, Europe was in turmoil with the Spanish Civil War at its height and Austria swallowed up into Hitler's Greater Germany – who also took over the cream of their players. The format remained a direct knock-out. Italy beat hosts France in the quarter-finals where Brazil also beat Czechoslovakia in a replay. But the Brazilians paid the price for over-confidence in their semi-final against Italy, resting star striker Leonidas, to keep him fresh for the Final. But Italy won 2–1, and they faced Hungary, who had thrashed Sweden 5–1 in the other semi-final. Hungary played the better football in the Final but lacked the vital finishing punch. Italy led 3–1 at half-time and ran out 4–2 winners thanks to two goals each from centre-forward Silvio Piola and left-winger Gino Colaussi.

Pele, aged only 17, celebrates one of his two sensational goals for Brazil in the 1958 World Cup Final against hosts Sweden.

GIUSEPPE MEAZZA
ITALY

Born: 23 August 1910 **Position:** Inside forward

Giuseppe Meazza, Italy's captain in 1938, was his country's first great attacker. He, and inside-forward partner Giovanni Ferrari, were the only two players to play in both the 1934 and 1938 World Cup Finals. Born in Milan, Meazza played for Internazionale, before moving to Milan – the stadium the two great clubs share is named for him. In international football, Meazza scored 33 times in 53 appearances for Italy, including two goals on his debut against Switzerland in 1930.

1950
BRAZIL

The first post-World-War-2 tournament was held in 1950 in Brazil – who built the world's biggest stadium for the event, the 200,000-capacity Maracana in Rio de Janeiro. England appeared for the first time in a finals whose format reverted to the mini-leagues system. Holders Italy, weakened by the loss of half-a-dozen top players in the Turin air crash the previous year, went out in the first round – as did England, shatteringly beaten 1–0 by the USA. Brazil, Uruguay, Sweden and Spain qualified for the concluding group in which the last game, between Brazil and Uruguay, was the effective Final. Brazil needed only a draw to become champions but Uruguay had other ideas. They survived the initial Brazilian whirlwind and hit back to win 2–1 with goals from Juan Schiaffino and Alcides Ghiggia.

1954
SWITZERLAND

The 1954 finals in Switzerland were expected to witness the formal crowning of Hungary as world champions, led by the great Ferenc Puskas. Instead they produced perhaps the greatest shock of all time as Hungary fell at the last hurdle to West Germany. The Germans had been thrashed 8–3 by Hungary in the first round mini-leagues, but they had fielded a team of reserves, confident that they could concede the match and still reach the quarter-finals – which they did. The quarter-finals saw two games, memorable for different reasons: Austria beat Switzerland

JUAN SCHIAFFINO
URUGUAY

Born: 28 July 1925 **Position:** Centre-forward

Juan "Pepe" Schiaffino was the first superstar of the post-war era. The slim, delicate playmaking Uruguayan centre-forward made his international debut as a 20-year-old at the Copa America and led his country to their shock victory at the 1950 World Cup. After starring at the 1954 World Cup, Schiaffino was sold by his club Peñarol to Italians Milan for a world record fee of £72,000.

FRITZ WALTER
WEST GERMANY

Born: 31 October 1920 **Position:** Inside-forward

Fritz Walter's international career began with a hat-trick in Germany's 9–2 rout of Romania in July 1940, and ended in the 1958 World Cup semi-finals, 61 matches and 33 goals later. The inside-forward and his centre-forward brother Ottmar, played together in the 1954 World Cup Final, when West Germany shocked Hungary 3–2, with Fritz as captain. Walter retired briefly, but returned at age 37 for the World Cup four years later. He played his entire club career at Kaiserslautern.

7–5 in a 12-goal thriller and Hungary overcame Brazil 4–2 in the so-called "Battle of Berne" when three players were sent off. By contrast, Hungary's 4–2 semi-final defeat of Uruguay was rated the finest game of football ever played. The Final was equally dramatic. Hungary stormed 2–0 ahead in the first eight minutes, then relaxed and lost 3–2. Helmut Rahn's late winner condemned Hungary to their first defeat in four years – in the match which mattered most.

1958
SWEDEN

Pele, aged 17, exploded onto the World Cup scene in Sweden. He missed the opening two group games through injury but then

that French forward Just Fontaine set a record which still stands by scoring 13 goals in the finals.

1962
CHILE

GARRINCHA
(Manoel Francisco dos Santos)
BRAZIL
Born: 28 October 1933 **Position:** Outside-right

If FIFA's present disciplinary process had been in force in 1962, Garrincha, Brazil's bow-legged outside right, would have missed the World Cup Final in Chile. He was sent off in the semi-final but was allowed to play in the Final. He had torn defences to shreds in the 1958 World Cup finals, but he rose to new heights as Brazil retained the trophy. The "Little Bird" drew on all his unpredictable genius after Pele was injured early in the tournament. He scored two superb goals to beat England in the quarter-finals, and the winner in the semi-final against Chile.

Chile were the hosts of the 1962 World Cup finals and they enjoyed a surprisingly successful tournament, reaching the semi-final. In fact, they and Brazil were the only two non-European nations to reach the last eight. England were undone by a dazzling performance from Garrincha, Chile saw off the Soviet Union, Yugoslavia defeated West Germany, while Czechoslovakia, runners-up back in 1934, reached the last four by overcoming Hungary. In the semi-finals, the defending champions were too good for the hosts, while the Czechs knocked out Yugoslavia. In the Final in Santiago. Czechoslovakia scored first through midfield general Josef Masopust, but Brazil – even without Pele – were on a different plane. They had even discovered a new goalscoring hero in Amarildo, who scored twice in a crucial first-round win over Spain and then snatched another cheeky goal in the Final. Goals from Vava and Zito ensured that the Czechs were left with silver medals for the second time.

1966
ENGLAND

Geoff Hurst became the only player to score a hat-trick in a World Cup Final when the Jules Rimet Trophy returned to European hands in the home of football. England's 4–2

GEOFF HURST
ENGLAND
Born: 8 December 1941 **Position:** Centre-forward

Geoff Hurst came into the England World Cup team when Jimmy Greaves was injured in the first round. After scoring the quarter-final winner against Argentina, he completed a perfect hat-trick (goals with each foot and his head) in the Final. A bustling centre-forward, Hurst was a big-game player with his goalscoring average in cup-ties for England, West Ham and Stoke City far outstripping his record in more mundane matches.

mesmerized Russia, Wales, France and Sweden in exhilarating succession as Brazil secured the first of their record four World Cups. It was the first time a country won the Cup outside of their own FIFA confederation. The tournament now settled into a format of four-team groups in the first round, followed by knock-out rounds. For the first and only time all four British home nations qualified. Scotland and England – albeit after a play-off – fell in the first round, but Northern Ireland reached the quarter-finals before crashing 4–0 to France, while Wales went down, by only 1–0 to Brazil, at the same stage, as Pele scored what he later described as one of the most important goals of his entire career. He went on to score twice more in the 5–2 Final thrashing of Sweden. Europe's only consolation was

PELE (Edson Arantes do Nascimento)
BRAZIL
Born: 21 October 1940 **Position:** Inside-forward

Considered by many to be the greatest ever player, Pele burst onto the World Cup scene at the age of 17 in 1958. Omitted from the team for the opening two group games, he did not score against Russia, but got one against Wales, three against France and two against hosts Sweden in the Final as Brazil secured their first World Cup. He was injured during the finals as Brazil retained the trophy in 1962, but was back to his imperious best in 1970. He retired after scoring more than 1,000 goals in senior football for Brazil and club sides Santos and New York Cosmos.

Geoff Hurst shoots the most controversial World Cup Final goal in history – England's third in 1966 against West Germany.

Record man Jairzinho turns to celebrate after scoring his country's third goal of the 1970 Final when Brazil defeated Italy 4–1 at the Azteca Stadium in Mexico City.

extra-time victory over West Germany also earned a knighthood for manager Alf Ramsey as well as places in football legend not only for Hurst but also for skipper Bobby Moore and Manchester United's Bobby Charlton. Yet England found goals scarce in the first round, being held goalless in the opening match by Uruguay and beating both Mexico and France "only" 2–0 apiece. There were no such problems for West Germany. A brilliant youngster named Franz Beckenbauer inspired a five-goal show first time out against Switzerland. Brazil were kicked out of the tournament by ruthless Bulgaria and Portugal while Italy succumbed to an amazing 1–0 upset against North Korea who nearly repeated the medicine against Portugal in the quarter-finals. Portugal went 3–0 down before recovering to win 5–3 and go on to achieve their best-ever third place thanks to the nine-goal power-shooting of Eusebio.

1970
MEXICO

Brazil soared to new heights as they claimed their historic World Cup hat-trick in Mexico. The heat and rarified atmosphere took its toll on Europe's main challengers but suited the Brazilians ideally. This was probably their greatest team, inspired by not only right-winger Jarzinho – a worthy successor to Garrincha – but by skipper and right-back Carlos Alberto, centre-forward Tostao, playmaker Gerson and the majestic Pele. They won all their six matches, scoring 19 goals, completed by a 4–1 crushing of Italy in the Final. Along the way, West Germany had taken dramatic revenge over England for 1966 when they recovered from 2–0 down to knock-out the holders by 3–2 in the quarter-finals. The semi-finals then saw the

Germans feature in an even greater contest which they lost 4–3 to Italy, also in extra-time. Italy, mentally and physically drained, were then no match in the Final for Brazil who tore the Italians' renowned *catenaccio* defence to shreds.

JAIRZINHO (Jair Ventura Filho)
BRAZIL

Born: 25 December 1944 **Position:** Right-winger

JAIRZINHO became the first player to score in every one of the winners' World Cup finals matches in 1970. He scored twice against Czechoslovakia in a first-round match and once each in the other five matches, including the only goal against England and the back-breaking third of the Final against Italy. Growing up, Jairzinho's hero was fellow right-winger Garrincha. He succeeded him in the Botafogo team and was a team-mate at the 1966 World Cup.

1974
WEST GERMANY

West Germany hosted the 1974 competition but, like England eight years earlier, had a rather stuttering ride through the first round, including a 1–0 loss to East Germany in a match of greater political significance than football as both teams had already qualified

FRANZ BECKENBAUER
WEST GERMANY
Born: 11 September 1945
Position: Midfield/sweeper

Franz Beckenbauer appeared to have achieved the ultimate when he led hosts West Germany to victory in his home Olympic stadium in Munich. "Kaiser Franz" captained his country, creatively revolutionizing the role of sweeper, but his Midas touch knew no bounds, even after retiring as a player. He went on coach West Germany to win the World Cup in 1990 and then – as an equally successful diplomat – "won" hosting rights for his country to the 2006 finals.

for the next stage. Instead of a straight knock-out from the quarter-final stage, eight teams advanced to play in a second group stage, the winners contesting the Final. The West Germans strode imperiously through this stage, but were still underdogs in the Final against a Dutch team that had swept all before them with their own, revolutionary style of "total football". Holland, inspired by Johan Cruyff, went ahead in only the second minute of the Final. Johan Neeskens converted the first-ever penalty-kick awarded in the Final before any West German player had even touched the ball. But the Germans, thanks to a penalty equaliser of their own from Paul Breitner, and a typically opportunist strike from "Der Bomber", Gerd Müller, won their second World Cup 20 years after the first. Poland – qualifying conquerors of England – surprisingly beat Brazil in the third place play-off.

Franz Beckenbauer grasps the new World Cup trophy as West Germany' winning captain in 1974 – unaware that he would also become the winning coach in 1990.

1978
ARGENTINA

Argentina both hosted and won the World Cup for the first time in 1978, defeating Holland 3–1 after extra time in the Final. Holland thus finished runners-up for the second successive tournament – badly missing the inspiration of Johan Cruyff who had quit the national team scene after

MARIO KEMPES
ARGENTINA
Born: 15 July 1952 **Position:** Striker

Mario Kempes was the only foreign player recalled for duty by coach Cesar Luis Menotti for the 1978 finals. But he was also the most decisive choice – top-scoring with six goals, including two in the Final in which Argentina defeated Holland 3–1 after extra-time. Kempes played in three World Cup finals, but failed to score in 11 appearances in 1974 and 1982 – the latter tournament being played in Spain where, with Valencia, he had enjoyed a lengthy club career.

leading them successfully through the qualifying section. England failed to qualify for the second successive finals, leaving the British banner to be flown by Scotland. They narrowly missed out on a second round slot despite beating Holland 3–2 in their last group match. Argentina were swept to victory not only by the goals of Valencia striker Mario Kempes but courtesy of a powerful and intimidating wave of home support plus the ruthless leadership of skipper and central defender Daniel Passarella. Brazil defeated Italy, and their new hero Paolo Rossi, 2–1 in the third-place play-off.

1982
SPAIN

Italy emulated Brazil and achieved their own World Cup hat-trick in 1982, defeating West Germany 3–1 in the Final in Spain. Another change in the format saw a semi-final stage added after the second groups. Rehabilitated striker Paolo Rossi was Italy's hero. He netted a hat-trick in a marvellous 3–2 second-round defeat of Brazil and then scored the opening

PAOLO ROSSI
ITALY
Born: 23 September 1956 **Position:** Striker

Paolo Rossi's career was one of peaks and troughs. Discarded by Juventus as a teenager, he starred at the 1978 World Cup finals, but found himself suspended from football in 1980 for his alleged part in a match-fixing scandal, only to repay the faith of coach Enzo Bearzot, who selected him for the squad after just three games back. Rossi led his country to World Cup glory in 1982, scoring six goals in Italy's last three matches. Within four years, injuries had put him out of football.

goal in the Final in Madrid. Argentina fell in the second round after Diego Maradona had been sent off against Brazil, who were the most attractive side on view. But not even the talents of Zico and Socrates could make up for fatal weaknesses in an overstretched defence. England and Northern Ireland both reached the second group stage, the latter after a shock win over the hosts in Valencia. The semi-finals saw the first-ever penalty shoot-out in World Cup finals history when West Germany defeated France after a dramatic 3–3 extra-time draw in Seville.

1986
MEXICO

Diego Maradona was both hero and villain when Mexico hosted the World Cup finals for the second time in 1986. Colombia were the original hosts, but they pulled out in 1983 for economic reasons and Mexico stepped in, despite suffering a massive earthquake in 1985. The tournament was expanded to 24 nations, with 16 teams advancing to knock-out rounds which replaced the second group stage. Maradona inspired Argentina to

DIEGO MARADONA
ARGENTINA

Born: 30 October 1960 **Position:** Striker

His country's captain, as well as the team's inspiration, Diego Maradona was hailed as the greatest natural talent since Pele. His career reached a peak at the 1986 finals in Mexico, when he scored two of the greatest individual goals ever seen on the world stage, against England and Belgium, in the quarter- and semi-finals respectively. Sadly, the pressure of superstardom told on him and his career and private life deteriorated into drug-induced chaos.

ultimate victory, albeit amid controversy. In the quarter-final against England, Maradona punched one of the World Cup's most notorious goals. Later in the same match, then in the semi-final against Belgium, he displayed the other side of his talent by scoring two of the finest individual goals in World Cup history. In the Final against West Germany, José Luis Brown and Jorge Valdano gave Argentina a 2–0 lead. Maradona was well-policed by Lothar Matthäus, but after the Germans had drawn level with late goals from Karl-Heinz Rummenigge and Rudi Völler, Maradona sent away Jorge Burruchaga for the winner.

1990
ITALY

The 1990 World Cup finals returned to Italy after 56 years, but they will go down, however, as one of the most negatively depressing in history. The overall impression

LOTHAR MATTHÄUS
WEST GERMANY

Born: 21 March 1961 **Position:** Midfield/sweeper

Lothar Matthäus was the antithesis of Diego Maradona. He was a pragmatic, hard-working, 90-minute midfield general and later sweeper who inspired his men more through energy than electricity. He had kept Maradona relatively quiet in the 1986 finals, but scored four times in the 1990 tournament, including a magnificent effort against Yugoslavia. Matthäus's international career stretched from 1980 to 2000, encompassing a world-record 150 caps and five World Cups.

Paolo Rossi goes past Brazil's Junior (6) during Italy's second round match in which Rossi scored a hat-trick – and Italy completed a hat-trick of World Cups with a 3–1 win in the Final.

Andreas Brehme (3) drives home Germany's World Cup-winning penalty, despite the best effort of Sergio Goycochea, in the 1990 Final against Argentina at the Stadio Olimpico in Rome.

was encapsulated in a gloomy Final in which Argentina had two players sent off before losing to West Germany on a controversial penalty. Lothar Matthäus was the Germans' designated penalty taker, but a muscle strain led to him stepping back when Rudi Völler went down in the box 10 minutes from time. Thus Andy Brehme wrote his name into history. Cameroon were the surprise of the finals – they defeated Argentina in the opening game despite finishing with only nine men – and only naïvety cost them a 3–2 defeat by England in extra time in the quarter-finals. Scotland's dreams of glory had effectively died with a 1–0 defeat in their opening game against debutants Costa Rica. England were also taken to extra time in the semi-finals by West Germany and lost on penalties after failures by Stuart Pearce and Chris Waddle.

1994
USA

FIFA took a huge gamble by awarding the 1994 World Cup to the USA – a country which did not have even a national outdoor 11-a-side league and which had last made a finals appearance in 1950. It proved to be an excellent decision. Brazil secured their record fourth World Cup success by defeating Italy in the first-ever penalty shoot-out in a Final. It was a disappointing end to an otherwise highly successful tournament in which the standard of football benefited

Opposite: *Zinedine Zidane, France's playmaker and two-goal hero mesmerizes Brazil's captain Dunga in the 1998 Final at the Stade de France.*

78

ROMARIO
(full name: Romario da Souza Faria)
BRAZIL
Born: 29 January 1966 **Position:** Striker

Romario, self-possessed king of Brazil's goal poachers, was both her five-goal top scorer and the event's finest player in the 1994 finals. After starring at the 1988 Olympic Games, scoring in the Final, and the 18-year-old moved to Europe. He made only one appearance in the 1990 World Cup, and had been in the international wilderness when recalled for the 1994 tournament. Romario then returned to play in Brazil. Injuries then robbed him of selection for the 1998 finals.

enormously from a refereeing crackdown. Diego Maradona grabbed the headlines again for the wrong reasons when he was expelled from the finals after failing a dope test. Reflecting the increasing power within the European game, seven of the eight quarter-finalists were European, but none of the four home nations qualified. The Republic of Ireland qualified again, and shocked Italy 1–0 in their opening game, but the goals of Roberto Baggio brought Italy through to the Final. Sadly, when it ended goalless after extra time, it was Baggio who missed the decisive penalty. Sweden took the bronze medals after defeating Hristo Stoichkov-inspired Bulgaria 4–0 in the third place play-off.

1998
FRANCE

Zinedine Zidane returned home from club exile in Italy with Juventus to present hosts

France with their first World Cup success. It was a long overdue reward for France, considering her role in the creation of the event. Political pressures had led to the finals being expanded to 32 teams. Brazil – inspired by new hero Ronaldo – Italy, France, Nigeria, Holland, Germany, Romania and Argentina topped the first-round groups and only Nigeria and Romania then failed to make it to the quarter-finals. Argentina squeezed past England in a second-round penalty shoot-out despite a wonder goal from new English starlet Michael Owen. Croatia, appearing in their first finals, finished third, defeating Holland 2–1 in the bronze medal play-off, and boasted the finals' top-scorer, thanks to Davor Suker's six goals. Brazil, for whom Ronaldo played amid huge controversy after collapsing earlier in the day, rarely threatened France in the Final. Zidane headed home twice from corners and Emmanuel Petit ran half the length of the pitch to extend the margin to a deserved 3–0 in the closing minutes.

ZINEDINE ZIDANE
FRANCE
Born: 23 June 1972 **Position:** Midfielder

There is a strong case to be made that Zinedine Zidane, who became the world's most expensive footballer in 2001, is France's greatest ever player, ahead even of Michel Platini. Zidane matched Platini's Euro Championship victory, but did better on the world stage, scoring twice in the 1998 World Cup Final. His performances at France 98 undoubtedly lifted the hosts to the ultimate level. Born in Marseille of Algerian descent, Zidane is a two-time FIFA World Footballer of the Year.

PICTURE ACKNOWLEDGEMENTS

The two faces of Korea: the modern Debec Plaza in Daegu (left) presents a contrasting image to the ancient temple in Suwon; both cities will host World Cup 2002 matches.

The publishers would like to thank the following sources for their kind permission to reproduce the pictures in this book:

Allsport UK Ltd 34/ Al Bello 45; Shaun Botterill 6b, 7t, 13tl, 13ml, 13mr, 26, 52, 53, 65; Clive Brunskill 5, 29; Stanley Chou 7t; Robert Cianflone 11ml, 80 l; Stu Foster 37; Stuart Franklin 24; Javier Garcia 61; Laurence Griffith 20–1; Mike Hewitt 59; Ross Kinnaird 47, 68; Nick Laham 27; David Leah 19, 22; Alex Livesey 23; Jamie McDonald 62; Craig Prentis 28; Gary M Prior 16, 25, 33; Ben Radford 1, 3, 8, 30, 32, 38, 40, 41, 63, 64, 69; Michael Steele 48, 50; Mark Thompson 6tr, 36; Martin Venegas 39, 60

Action Images/ Stuart Franklin 4; Richard Heathcote 43, 57; Rudy Lhomme 44; John Sibley 54, 55; Darren Walsh 58

Colorsport 78/ Varley 75

Empics Ltd/ Matthew Ashton 2, 7b, 11br, 11tl, 12b, 12tr, 13bl, 56; Adam Davy 35, 46; Mike Egerton 49; Paul Marriott 67; Tony Marshall 31, 66; Steve Mitchell 9; Peter Robinson 76, 77; Neal Simpson 42; Simon Wilkinson 79

Getty Images/ Photodisc 80r

Hulton Archive 70, 73br

Popperfoto 51, 71, 72–3, 74